DEC - 2001

WAY
OUT
WEST

WAY
OUT
WEST

ON THE TRAIL OF AN ERRANT ANCESTOR

MICHAEL SHAW BOND

M&S

National Library of Canada Cataloguing in Publication Data

Bond, Michael Shaw
    Way out west : on the trail of an errant ancestor

Includes bibliographical references.
ISBN 0-7710-1132-6

1. Bond, Michael Shaw – Journeys – Canada, Western.   2. Milton, William Fitzwilliam, Viscount, 1839–1877.   3. Prairie Provinces – Description and travel.   4. British Columbia – Description and travel.   5. Canada, Western – History.   I. Title.

FC3205.4.B65 2001   917.1204'1   C2001-901126-1
F1060.B72 2001

Unless otherwise noted, quotations are from William Fitzwilliam Viscount Milton and W. B. Cheadle, *The North-West Passage by Land*, London, Cassell, Petter and Galpin, 1865.

We acknowledge the financial support of the Government of Canada through the Book Publishing Industry Development Program for our publishing activities. We further acknowledge the support of the Canada Council for the Arts and the Ontario Arts Council for our publishing program.

Designed by: Ingrid Paulson
Typeset in Minion by M&S, Toronto
Printed and bound in Canada

McClelland & Stewart Ltd.
The Canadian Publishers
481 University Avenue
Toronto, Ontario
M5G 2E9
www.mcclelland.com

1 2 3 4 5   05 04 03 02 01

This book is dedicated to my grandmother
Myrtle Violet Willis
(1909–1998)

CONTENTS

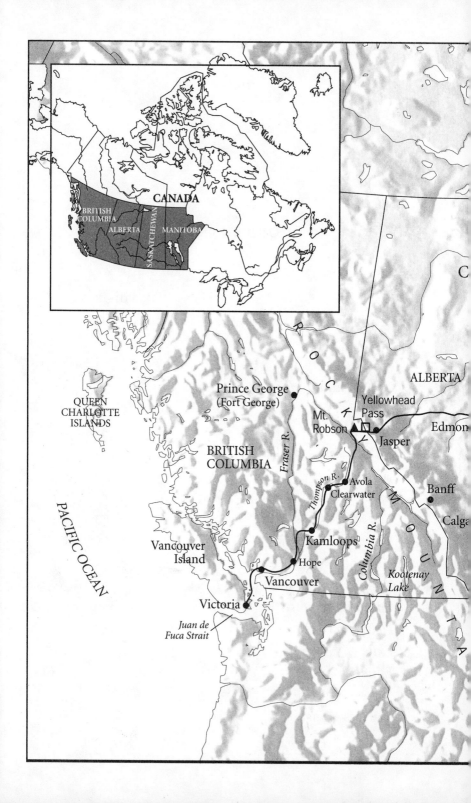

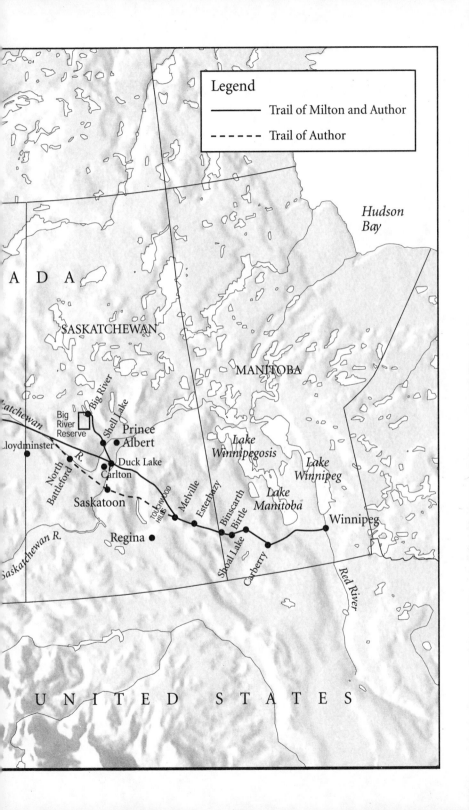

ACKNOWLEDGEMENTS

Many people have helped me and I am indebted to them. Those I would particularly like to thank include, in Canada: Bernard, Carolyn, Robert, Richard, Jonathan and Stephanie Lalonde, for their kindness and great help at Morin (Devil's) Lake and the Big River Reserve; Alexander Dietz, for his expertise on the Cree; David LaChance at Big River; Stewart and Grace Shackell in Ottawa; Dave and Chris of Skyline Trail Rides in Jasper; Steve, Moe and Len at Austin, Manitoba; Dan and Alba Palsich at Paradise Hill; Ida at the Yellowhead Museum in Clearwater, B.C.; John Staunton at the Canadian Museum of Civilization in Ottawa; Michael Eamon at the National Archives of Canada in Ottawa; and Professor Jock Murray at Dalhousie University.

And in England: Martyn Johnson, who opened more doors for me around Wentworth than anyone; Patrick Scott and Camilla Edwards, for reading and correcting the first draft of the book; Francis and Natalie Phillimore, with whom I learnt how to look after horses; Ruth Harman at Sheffield Archives; Joan Jones at Royal Doulton; Dr. Robert Mahler at the Royal College of Physicians; John Teesdale; Roy Young; Mrs. John Cheadle; May Bailey; Lady Juliet Tadgell; Annabel Hardman, for helping me get my lucky break; Maggie Noach and Simon Moore; Polly, for her support early on; Richard Wolman, for inspiration; Robert and Sabina ffrench Blake, for their encouragement and many suppers; Pat Kennedy, my editor at McClelland & Stewart; and Bill Hamilton at A. M. Heath, who persuaded them to publish this book.

Thank you to my mother and all my family at home for keeping me going, to my uncle Ian, to my aunt Juliette for her help with Grandma's papers, to my second cousin Lady Barbara Ricardo, and to aunt Chris for grand days on Vancouver Island.

WAY
OUT
WEST

PROLOGUE

When I was sixteen my grandmother gave me my first
driving lesson. She was half blind and she had not driven
since guiding her old Volvo through a hedge into a field of
ripening wheat. In her view this did not make her any less
qualified. As she kept pointing out, it was her hedge and her
wheat. She considered learning to drive a rite of passage and
if anyone was going to instil in me bad road habits it was
going to be her. Needless to say the lesson had little to do
with the Highway Code. It ended against the wall of her
kitchen with an inverted bumper. Grandma was delighted. It
had all gone according to plan.

My grandmother loved dramas. Any story that came her
way she would exaggerate before passing on. My mother
would hear things about me or my brother or sisters that

would make her frantic, only to discover they were mostly the products of Grandma's imagination.

She lived on her farm in Hampshire surrounded by people who had worked for her for decades and would have followed her anywhere. Some of them had come down with her from Scotland when my grandfather Stanley died after the war, and Hampshire was the furthest by several hundred miles that they had been from home. They were all part of her family, which went beyond blood ties, and she treated them thus, upholding archaic traditions such as providing each with a turkey at Christmas. Near her death, when she was completely blind and really too ill for anything except lying in bed, she insisted on being dressed each morning and sat in her chair in the kitchen in time to greet "the ladies," as she called them – her cleaners – and talk with them over coffee, a ritual she had enacted every morning of the past fifty years and which she would skip, well, over her dead body.

Grandma had seen something of life and suffering. Stanley was sixty – twice her age – when they married, a highly successful businessman who had built the Butterworths publishing company and was rather set in the ways of a single man. During the Second World War he installed Grandma in a lonely castle on the banks of the River Dee in Scotland "for her safekeeping," and this was where my father and uncle were born. When they were still babies Stanley died of leukemia and she moved to Hampshire and brought them up herself. My father died of cancer when he was thirty-nine. I was thirteen, too young to know him properly, so thereafter every time I saw her Grandma would make a special effort to indulge me with a story about Dad and his childhood – embellished, of course. After Stanley died she married again, an insurance man called David Willis, and she outlived him too. I always wondered, and I could never bring myself to ask, how Grandma managed to cope with the deaths of two husbands and a son.

There were few things I looked forward to more than hearing Grandma tell her stories. Visiting her was the high point of every weekend. It was best to arrive around tea-time because she would have been drinking whisky and milk since eleven in the morning and the stories flowed more easily with that. She would always instruct her helper to lace my tea with whisky. And there would be scones, freshly made and disguised by cream. There was no better way to spend an afternoon.

It wasn't just the stories that Grandma told, it was the way she told them. There she would be in her red armchair, propped up by cushions with large dark glasses over her sightless eyes, like an officiating guru at an invocation of deities. When she heard you come in she would greet you with an expansive "Darling" with all the emphasis on the *Dar*, or with "Oh My Dear" with the stress on the *Dear*, and so much enthusiasm it made you feel she had been waiting for you for days. Then you would go over and kiss her and she would take your hand and hold it for ages and fuss over you while you sat down and made ready to listen. Since she could no longer use her eyes she did other things to accentuate a point, swaying like a priest administering the sacrament, grandly nodding her head. Her pronunciation and choice of words were so correct and old-fashioned that you felt you had been swept back to the Victorian age. A car was always a motor-car. "Gone" sounded like "gorn." She loved extravagant adjectives. A distracting noise was a "God-Almighty" din. She made frequent use of words like "splendid." All this made her storytelling deeply ritualistic. Whenever we tried to retell her stories to someone else they never felt the same.

We had heard most of them several times over. One of our favourites was of when she tried to disperse her beloved father's ashes over his garden. She could not quite bring herself to do it, so instructed his faithful gardener: "Windsor, would you mind frightfully scattering the Colonel in the raspberries?" But the story that fired me most was about her grandfather, William Milton, eldest son of the sixth Earl Fitzwilliam, who thanks to Grandma's storytelling had become something of a legend in our family. "He was an adventurer," she said. "A wild, wild man. My dear, I never knew him, but they say he was fearless. Not at all like the rest of the Fitzwilliams. He was different, you see."

So different, in fact, that he had become a celebrity in late nineteenth-century England after travelling for two years across Canada by canoe and horseback, suffering disease, starvation, Indians and bears to map a route from the Atlantic to the Pacific. "He died in Canada, you know, he and my grandmother together, somewhere out in the wild. My mother was an orphan at the age of two." Sometimes she would bring out his book about the journey, *The North-West Passage by Land*, extravagantly bound in red leather. It had pictures, including one showing Milton with Dr. Cheadle, his redoubtable travelling companion, and a group of Indians. Milton's hair was as long as the Indians' and he was wearing a red headband and could for all the world have been a Native himself.

Every time Grandma told the story of Milton's journey it varied a little. I had no idea how much of it was truth and how much myth, or which parts were exaggerated. Not that it mattered. Most of my boyhood fantasies involved wild animals and heroic survival against the odds in a mythic wilderness and here was an ancestor who had actually lived them, an adventurer-hero of my own blood. I was hardly going to let a little fiction (or truth) get in the way. I wondered how heirs to vast earldoms – the Fitzwilliams in Milton's day owned most of south Yorkshire – were supposed to have behaved in those days. Not as he had, I was sure. Grandma reckoned he was a rebel, "like me, my dear." I was hooked.

I don't remember how many times I made Grandma tell me the story but she never tired of it. The fact that her sister, my great-aunt Crystal, was living in Canada west of the Rockies close to where Milton came out of the wilderness made it all the more tantalizing. Grandma said it was because of him and the stories about him that Crystal emigrated there after the Second World War.

Aunt Chris, as she likes to be called, came over from Canada every October for her sister's birthday. This was always exciting because she is even more eccentric than Grandma. There was pandemonium in the house for the two weeks she was there. Bizarre things happened. One day she took everyone off to an East Indian christening, and it was considered no coincidence when that night my step-grandfather David fell two floors from his bedroom window and landed on his head in the flower bed. Apart from a broken wrist and a headache he was unscathed, but the rumour stuck that the christening was to blame. "That was quite a night," Grandma recalled. "We never really knew what made him fall out the window. We had the most extraordinary food at the christening and it may have had something to do with that. The police came to find out what had happened and I know they thought I'd pushed him."

Another year a notoriously unstable local woman appeared at Grandma's house and started banging on the front door claiming she had been cheated by the farm in some way. Aunt Chris let her in and calmed her down and sent her away, but not before David had called the police. When the officer arrived Aunt Chris opened the door to him. Convinced the woman before him was the hysteric he had been assigned to apprehend, he bundled my great-aunt into the back of his van "with everything but handcuffs" and took her to the police station.

While Grandma said that her sister moved to Canada because of Milton, Aunt Chris said it was because she hated her mother, and the only person she knew overseas was her nanny's daughter in Quebec. She is vitriolic about her mother, Theresa Fitzwilliam, who was Milton's third and youngest daughter. "That woman would be behind bars for cruelty to children if she were alive today." She says her mother once hit her so hard for not curtseying to a visitor that she split her skull. Grandma, who was ten years older, was like a surrogate parent to her sister. She seemed to get on better with their mother, though she remembered her as "quite tough and hard. I think she was disappointed that I wasn't a boy."

Aunt Chris knows *The North-West Passage by Land* intimately. Her sons, like Milton's, were born in Canada. She has had her fair share of adventure, especially during the war, when she parachuted out of a burning plane over France, was held hostage by a crazed GI in an ambulance she was driving in London and got imprisoned by the Russians for three weeks on mistaken identity after taking a wrong turning near Berlin. She never was any good at reading maps. Her first job in Canada was making tea for hundreds of lumberjacks in a loggers' camp in Quebec. It struck me that Aunt Chris, unwittingly or not, had already followed in Milton's footsteps. She was set to become the family folk hero for the next generation.

It was while Aunt Chris was staying for the last time that Grandma and I hatched our plan. In honour of her heroic grandfather whom she had never met, I would follow Milton's path across Canada, on horseback, crossing the Rockies through the pass that he had mapped and ending my journey on Aunt Chris's doorstep. It was more of a dream, really, because I had never even sat on a horse. But we talked about it as if I were going to do it, and Grandma began to alarm my mother with stories of unsurvivable Canadian winters and how bears could pull people off galloping horses. Sometimes she pretended to disapprove herself. "Darling, it's a splendid idea, but I know I'll get the blame when the bears get you." Her vision of the Canadian wilderness became ever more outrageous. One day she announced that, as if the bears weren't bad enough, there were African lions out there too. Grandma was really enjoying herself.

In the months before she died she became very weak and sometimes she was only half-conscious. "Am I there?" she kept asking, as if wondering herself which world she were in. Her doctor would shake his head and mutter that most people would have gone weeks ago, but Grandma was the bravest fighter I knew and she would not let go. She found it hard to talk, and we found it hard to get through to her, and she would not register unless we took her hand. Yet sometimes, even in this difficult state, there were flashes of that indomitable character – the delight in her weak voice when she realized who you were, a sudden demand for tea.

Perhaps this was what she had inherited from her grandfather: an unbreakable spirit that kept him going in his wilderness and was keeping Grandma going in hers. Perhaps she empathized with him more than she let on and this was why she had so celebrated his memory and carefully passed it on to me. So when she died in her bed at home aged eighty-eight one Tuesday morning in July and many months later than every doctor had predicted, it was as much in her memory as Milton's that I promised myself I would follow the great plan we had hatched together. Here were two family heroes worthy of remembering.

OF MYTHS AND MEN

There is nobody alive who remembers Milton but there are those who remember his children. My great-grandmother, Theresa Evelyn Vilunza, was the youngest. Grandma said she was hard; Grandma's sister, Aunt Chris, says "hard" is a considerable understatement. My uncle remembers her as a grand old lady who would never talk to the servants, a singular personality and hugely loved. A "society lady." Each of these opinions is sincerely held and each derived from a particular standpoint – a woman loved or feared or both depending on whose view you sought. Such are the vagaries of kinship. One thing on which they all agree is that she became bitter towards the end of her life after my great-grandfather lost all his money in the 1929 stock exchange crash. She separated from him because he could not keep her in the ways to which she was accustomed. She is buried so far from the other graves in her churchyard in Sussex that she is practically in a field. "She didn't want to be near anyone," said Grandma. She had high standards, my great-grandmother. When she was twenty she placed an advertisement for a husband in the *Irish Times* that my grandmother reckoned was only partly a spoof:

> "Wanted – By a Lady Who wishes to be married – immediately if not sooner – a young Gentleman of Prepossessing appearance (Rosy Cheeks, Blue eyes & oily Curly Black Hair Preferred). Must be unable to ride but prepared to provide Hunters for his wife & her Friends. Must be of an Intensely affectionate disposition & Devotedly fond of Sun-sets. Must be over 4ft 2" & Sound. To an eligible "Parti" a month's Honeymoon (before Hunting) will be granted but the Lady does not guarantee to accompany him – all applications with Photographs of the applicants to be sent to Wentworth."

Wentworth – short for Wentworth Woodhouse – was the family home in Yorkshire and the longest house in Europe. Grandma did not know how many young gentlemen applied but she reckoned her mother would have had a few to choose from.

Laura, Milton's eldest child, was also "formidable," according to her daughter-in-law Celia Douglas. His second child, Mabel, was a Labour supporter – controversial in a house of Liberals – and beloved around Wentworth for her charity work and her eccentric habits, her determination and her battered old raincoat and string bag of vegetables. That leaves Billy. Everyone remembers Billy, Milton's son and heir. Charles Doyne, who was born in 1904 and is Milton's great-nephew, remembers him better than anyone, above all for his energy, his great life-loving personality, his attention to detail and concern that things should run just right, his passion for his cars and boats and his engineering skill. "He was a great and compassionate employer," recalls Charles. He was also a Boer and First World War hero, and ADC to the Marquess of Lansdowne, the Viceroy of India. In January 1896 the *Yorkshire Post* mistakenly reported that Billy – by then Lord Milton after his father's death – had been thrown from his horse and killed while crossing a bridge at Wentworth. It published an obituary and portrait under the headline: "Tragic Death of Lord Milton." Billy, when he saw it, declared: "I have never felt less like a dead man." Billy, says Charles Doyne, was a typical Fitzwilliam male.

Just as typical was his son Peter, Second World War soldier, who became eighth Earl when Billy died in 1943. "Full of life, full of living, full of laughter and full of drink," is how one of his ex-employees recalls him. "No one disliked him." Another remembers him, fondly, as a tearaway. And an engineer. And a womanizer. The plane crash that killed him also killed his lover Lady Kathleen Hartington, widow of the Duke of Devonshire's heir and sister of the future American president John F. Kennedy. Lady Juliet Tadgell, Peter's only child and the most significant Fitzwilliam inheritor living, was thirteen when he died. "The word I most often heard used about my father was 'charming,'" she says. "He was charming to everyone. He could talk to anyone."

How typical a Fitzwilliam was Milton? It is hard to say, because hardly anyone in the family knows anything about him. I tracked down all his forty-odd direct adult descendants and apart from my grandmother and great-aunt, only Lady Barbara Ricardo – one of his great-grandchildren – had anything to say about him. She called him "an exceptional engineer," and this at least is a talent he passed to his son and grandson.

I imagined that the family would have been proud of its explorer son. So where were the biographies, the photograph albums, the archived letters, the gilt-framed portraits and the relics of the Wild West? Charles Doyne says Billy never spoke of his father. Was he an embarrassment? Had he done something inexcusable? Was he a creation of my grandmother's imagination? I couldn't believe there was so little to go on. It was like trying to build an ancient invertebrate from its trace fossils. He has all but been blanked out of the family record. Had he not been the eldest son he would probably have dropped off the tree entirely, like the illegitimate Fitzwilliam offspring they talk about in the pubs around Wentworth. All rumours of the existence of this maverick greatly overblown. Remarkably for the heir to an earldom, even his will has disappeared.

Pondering this, I returned to where the story started – my grandmother's farmhouse. I walked through the silent rooms hoping for inspiration and spotted her old brown leather suitcase of letters, the fountainhead of many a family mystery. Inside was a letter from Milton as a boy addressed to his mother at Wentworth Woodhouse. It was sent from Avignon, where he was staying at a private tutor's:

> Please do let me know as soon as possible when you want me to come home for certain, and when and where we shall all be the next coming and midsummer hollydays, if you knew how I long for an answer I am sure you would send one directly. On 15th April I shall have been 3 months which was the greatest time you said I should stay and as I abominate being away here most throughly I really must come home then, and not go away again anywhere for an awfull long time except to Eton.

Not that this was much of a clue. It told me that he liked to write in superlatives, and that he was bad at spelling. My Eton housemaster, now the school's unofficial historian, looked him up in his records and concluded that his career at the school had been "decorous, but not illustrious" – in other words he had failed to distinguish himself in anything, sporting or academic. I immediately felt an empathy for him, as this was how one of my tutors had summed up my Eton career. I wondered if he had disliked the place as much as I had.

Next I tried the Fitzwilliam family archives in Sheffield. It is vast and there are files on just about every Fitzwilliam that lived. Milton's, predictably, is virtually empty: scraps of letters, notes from his secretary, drafts of speeches from his time in politics. But at the bottom of this file I found a small bundle of papers that would transform the way I looked at Milton. At first they resembled unpaid bills: lists of products and a signature, some numbers, his name at the top. But they turned out to be prescriptions for medicines, and not for the common cold: opium, lavender oil, belladonna, orange rind, chloral hydrate, strychnine, potassium bromide. Such sedatives and stimulants were common remedies at that time for epilepsy.

My conviction that Milton suffered from this disease (it is never mentioned by name in reference to him), and that this had much to do with the mystery surrounding his life, came from a collection of letters in a secondary Fitzwilliam archive in Northampton, near another of the family's estates at Milton Park. Most of the letters are from his childhood and many are about him being ill.

In October 1850, when he was eleven, his father wrote to his grandfather: "William may have to remain here longer than I had anticipated, as his health is not very settled, and he has had many but only slight attacks of unconsciousness. The Edinburgh doctors recommend quiet, and no amusement of an exciting tendency." Five years later, from Ireland: "I am sorry to say that William has had another attack like those he has had, but it was very much slighter, and there was only one, whereas he has had two on the previous occasions." And when he was eighteen: "William, I am happy to say is much better than when I left here three weeks ago, and I believe has had very little tendency towards a reversal of his old attacks and although he had tendencies when he first came here from London still those tendencies appear to be diminishing. He is evidently much stronger, and his face is fatter, and he does with far less medicine."

Epileptics in the nineteenth century were not exactly the toast of society and they had a lot of history against them. The ancient Greeks and Romans were so convinced that epilepsy was caused by demons or deities, or that it targeted those who had sinned against the Moon goddess Selene, that they referred to it as the Sacred Disease. To suffer it was a disgrace, and to make matters worse for sufferers it was thought to be contagious. A Hippocratic text called *On the Sacred Disease*, written around 410 BC, rejected any divine origin and instead blamed it on too much phlegm in the brain brought about by changes in temperature or in the direction of the wind – but such rationality was rare. People sought cures in the stars, or in magical rites, and later in Christian ones. The Greek doctor Alexander of Tralles recommended taking a nail from a wrecked ship, fashioning it into a bracelet, setting into it the bone from a stag's heart lifted from the animal while still alive, and wearing it on the left arm. Other common treatments included eating seal's genitals, drinking the blood of gladiators, wearing the root of the peony as an amulet and rubbing your feet with menstrual blood. The fourteenth-century surgeon Guy de Chauliac had epileptics write the names of the Three Wise Men on a piece of parchment in their own blood and recite three paternosters and three Ave Marias daily for three months. This from a doctor. Such was the ignorance in the medical profession about the illness in the Middle Ages that it was believed a mother could give it to her child simply by taking fright at seeing an epileptic person while she was pregnant.

At the start of the eighteenth century many doctors were still blaming demons and witches and prescribing human blood and bones. Julius Caesar, Emperor Caligula and Mohammed were recognized as epileptic and the disease became associated with prophecy and genius, but it was still frowned on. By the nineteenth century doctors had accepted it as a disease of the nervous system, though their suggestions as to what caused it were fanciful. Common explanations were masturbation, drunkenness, difficult menstruation, fright, fear, wrath, misery, dentition, a blow to the head, sudden chill, too much sun, and debauchery. The remedies of that era were similarly creative. As late as 1861 one of the foremost experts on epilepsy, Russell Reynolds, recommended a new trial of mistletoe. Cauterization on the head with a hot iron was popular, as was bloodletting, bowel-purging and trephining – drilling a hole in the skull. Silver nitrate was tried but severely poisoned some patients. Belgian doctors developed a way of artificially inducing a fever, which they thought might help, by half-undressing the patient and shutting him outside on an extremely cold day, then tucking him into a warm bed until he perspired.

Milton was lucky to get away with opium, sulphuric acid and strychnine, though strychnine is more likely to cause than prevent a fit. Cheadle, who was his personal doctor as well as his travelling companion in Canada, also prescribed him the most promising drug of the day, potassium bromide, which worked by depressing the central nervous system. Although its success was tempered by a high incidence of bromine poisoning it was clearly considered worth the risk. A doctor in New York, William Hammond, presented at a lecture a fourteen-year-old boy whom he had cured of epileptic attacks with the apology: "As you see he is broken down in appearance, has large abscesses in his neck, and is altogether in a bad condition. But this is better than to have epilepsy."

There are two kinds of epileptic fit, both involving electrical disorder in the brain. The *petit mal*, or partial seizure, involves a very brief loss of consciousness that might force the sufferer to stop what he is doing, but passes after a few moments, allowing him to continue. It is more a senselessness than a blackout and the person might not be aware of it and afterwards might, for example, continue a sentence he had begun to speak. The *grand mal* or generalized seizure involves the whole brain at once and a total loss of consciousness. The *grand mal* seems to have been Milton's ordeal:

> The patient, it may be without warning, utters a strange inarticulate cry, and falls suddenly to the ground insensible, as if struck by lightning. He usually has no time to save himself, but knocks against any object near him, and may thus receive serious injury, or he may fall into the fire, or into water. He becomes deadly pale, his body rigid, with the back arched and the features set, and he ceases to breathe. Soon the colour changes, the face becomes livid purple, the veins of the neck swell up and pulsate, the eyeballs

protrude, a gurgling sound is heard in the throat, and death seems imminent. But almost immediately breathing begins again, and the whole body is thrown into a series of successive convulsive twitchings or jerkings. The trunk and limbs are thrown about in various ways, the face is hideously contorted, the tongue jerked out between the teeth and often bitten, the jaws convulsed so that the teeth may be broken. A blood-stained foam escapes from the mouth. After about two or three minutes the jerkings cease, leaving the patient prostrate and comatose for a time. Then he may open his eyes, look around him with a dazed expression, and go to sleep. On awaking he is quite unconscious of what has happened. (Chambers's *Encyclopaedia*, 1895)

It is hard to know what might have caused Milton's epilepsy since even today 70 per cent of cases are unexplained. The commonest causes are head trauma, brain tumour, stroke, poisoning, a viral infection and injury or illness in the womb. Since his family never publicly acknowledged that he suffered the illness, I did not fancy my chances of finding out why. It could have been hereditary, though there were no epileptic Fitzwilliams before him or since – at least none admitted to.

It is easier to imagine how it must have affected him, in the absence of any decent anticonvulsant drug therapy. The nineteenth-century French psychiatrist Benedict Augustin Morel, who studied the lives and characters of epileptics in his asylum, maintained that virtually all sufferers were angry and irritable and that their irritability worsened the more they suffered, and that a few during or after their fits could be psychopathic. Several people who knew Milton remarked on his ill temper and his obstinacy, including Cheadle many times in his diary. It is hardly surprising he was angry given what he had to go through with his fits, random and unforewarned, and given how his epilepsy would have set him back in life. Then there were the mood swings to which his father alluded in one of his letters – the "great mental excitement followed by considerable depression of spirits." This too is common among epileptics, at least half of whom suffer significant psychological or social difficulties. Other psychoses associated with it are excessive anxiety, memory impairment, mental confusion, oversensitivity and hypochondria. Look hard enough and you can see all these in accounts of Milton's behaviour; but which are truly the result of his epilepsy and which facets of his natural character it is not safe to guess, and neither perhaps is it sensible. The illness was so much a part of him that Milton without epilepsy is another Milton entirely.

Such an illness today is hard enough to bear and it is still stigmatized, but in the nineteenth century how much harder? It was one thing to suffer it raw and untempered by modern drugs, but the most tragic thing must have been to know that everyone else thought you freakish, mentally imbalanced, antisocial, incurable, mad, possessed or simply frightening. Milton's family and friends might have been as suspicious and unsympathetic as anyone, especially given the aversion to such defects in aristocratic circles at that time and how poorly the illness was understood even by doctors.

Usually, the epileptic is avoided; on all faces he reads his sentence to isolation. Everywhere he goes, menacing and insurmountable obstacles arise to his obtaining a position, to his establishing himself, to his relationships, to his very livelihood; he must bid farewell his dreams of success. . . . This is death to the spirit. (From "Recherches et considerations relatives à la symptomatologie de l'épilepsie" by Billod in *Annales medico-psychologiques* 2, 1843).

People coped with it in different ways and Milton was lucky that he had money. A personal doctor must have made life a little more bearable.

My grandmother never mentioned Milton's epilepsy. Either she did not know or she was not saying. Nobody else mentioned it and nowhere is it spelled out. For some families, and the aristocracy especially, epilepsy was a great evil because it can be inherited and thus it was "in the blood." Impure blood was anathema to families for whom breeding and lineage were everything. In some families it still is. One Fitzwilliam descendant has assured me that I have got it wrong about Milton's illness, for "there can be no bad blood in our family."

Thus Milton had to bear not only the disease but also his family's embarrassment. Publicly he was simply "ill," or unavailable "on account of his health." The week before his twenty-seventh birthday, *The Times* announced: "We regret to state that Lord Milton is again so seriously ill that he is unable to leave town as soon as was expected, but it is hoped that in the course of a few days he will be sufficiently recovered to move to the seaside, in accordance with the advice of his medical attendants." Occasionally he or his family would feel compelled to publish a more elaborate excuse, such as the one that appeared in *The Times* in 1869 when he was too ill to attend the House of Commons: "Lord Milton, MP, has been obliged to withdraw temporarily from Parliamentary life in consequence of a severe attack of inflammation in the eyes, which required him to confine himself to a darkened room. His Lordship is progressing favourably towards recovery."

Most of the letters from his childhood and school and from Trinity College, Cambridge, mention his illness. The expression "on account of his health" comes up everywhere and on account of it he did not graduate from Cambridge. On the other hand neither did he officially enrol, which could mean he had no intention of graduating and used Cambridge as a finishing school, as many others of his background did. He was sent on tours around Europe for months in pursuit of a climate "more profitable to health." He was put on special diets, largely at the insistence of his grandfather, who wrote optimistically less than two months before his own death: "I hope the ups tendency to illness in William will go on – in medicine I have no great faith but I have great faith in diet which I hope will be enforced upon him systematically and perseveringly."

They tried everything. An undated letter from the family doctor to Earl Fitzwilliam contains a lock of his hair, presumably for analysis or the concoction of some alternative remedy. The doctor was not hopeful: "I see no prospect of all this business finishing. Dr. Willis saying that he can cure the thing appears to me very extraordinary." Milton had a personal doctor with him throughout his life. When choosing a suitable travelling companion for Canada, the fact that Cheadle was a friend of Milton's from Cambridge would probably have been secondary to his being a doctor. (Cheadle was also four years older and an oarsman of impressive build, which would have helped.) In this way were his days commanded by his illness.

The more I considered Milton's epilepsy and the mood of the age towards such a disease, the more it seemed to fit what I was piecing together of his character. From the few letters I had, and reports from local newspapers, it appears that his whole life was shaped by it. Certainly his illness, or the mood swings that accompanied it, had a drastic effect on his behaviour. On April 20, 1861, the *Globe* and the *Morning Post* in Yorkshire announced his impending marriage to Miss Dorcas Chichester, daughter of Lord Edward Chichester and niece of the third Marquis of Donegal. A week later the *Globe* retracted: "We are requested by Viscount Milton to state that a paragraph which appeared in our impression of Saturday relating to a matrimonial arrangement in which his Lordship's name is prominently mentioned, was wholly unauthorised." The *Morning Post* also backtracked, but merely said the rumour of his marriage was "premature." This was something of an under-statement. Milton had broken off the engagement, claiming that he had been misinformed over Miss Chichester's age, justifying this to her father in the following way:

> My Lord,
>
> I do distinctly complain that misrepresentations were made to me concerning your daughter's age, although it was well known that the disparity of years believed by my family to exist formed a serious objection to our marriage. I was in the first instance informed that she was "almost 20" – this in the presence of Lady Chichester and other members of your family. Subsequently Lady Chichester, although refusing to tell me the age, induced me to believe that she was 23. At the time when the census was taken I had reason to believe that Miss Chichester was 21. It is true that Mr Parker in a casual conversation expressed his belief that she was 25 years old. When in America I received a copy of the certificate of baptism of Miss Chichester which proved for the first time what her real age was. Your Lordship is incorrect in suppos-ing that certificate to be otherwise than genuine. The age shown in the certificate differs most noticeably from that given to me by the members of Miss Chichester's family.

Her real age was seventeen. It seemed a fantastic excuse. Had he simply changed his mind? Lord Chichester was appalled; he demanded Milton send back everything his daughter had given him, down to a missing page from her prayer book.

There is another possible scenario. Perhaps Milton had wanted to marry this girl but was forbidden by his family, and had been pressured by them into constructing his elaborate get-out clause to save them embarrassment. Consider the following letter to Lord Chichester from Milton's father:

> My son's conduct has been so unsteady and his health so bad that I do not feel justified in consenting to his taking upon himself the serious responsibility of a married life. I feel sure you will think with me that I should not be doing right in withholding from you these facts, a knowledge of which will probably drastically alter your judgment as to your daughter's prospects of happiness. My son suffers from fits which cause at times great mental excitement sometimes followed by considerable depression of spirits.

I imagined scenes of great distress played out in that household, talk of honour and ancient lineages and of the dishonour of disease, of noble sacrifice. I imagined the twenty-one-year-old Milton, son and heir, burdened by responsibility and his father's disappointment. I did a great deal of imagining and I could prove little of it, but I was getting a strong feeling for Milton that he had been rather cast off by his family and was a subject of shame for them.

He did, however, have a friend in a mysterious Mr. Teesdale, who signed his name as Lord Teesdale though there has never been such a title and who shared with Milton a disinclination to spell correctly. In a letter to Milton he congratulated him on breaking off the engagement and for being "free from those soft influences which are apt occassionally to occurrance. I shall have the great happiness of seeing you some day secured in that high position which once was risked so terribly."

"Lord" John Marmaduke Teesdale, it turns out, was Milton's solicitor, and "a bit of a rogue" according to his great-grandson, who shares all his names and whom I tracked down to an old country house in Gloucestershire. I wrote to him, and he invited me to lunch. When I arrived I rang the doorbell and, failing to rouse anyone, stepped inside. A small man sporting a sharp white beard and an elaborate purple shirt and neckerchief hurried past without noticing me. I pursued him into the house and caught up with him under a large wall hanging of the Teesdale family tree. It was John Marmaduke himself.

He is eighty-nine, wizened and wizard-like, fairly deaf and cunningly particular about what he hears. He is a successful portrait painter. He appears proud of his great-grandfather but will not intimate what of his character he has inherited. He showed me Marmaduke senior's photograph album, immaculately preserved. Inside are several pictures of Milton, though this did not necessarily indicate a close relationship. "I'm afraid my great-grandfather was rather a snob, and clients of his family firm tended, if they had titles, to qualify for the family album, often with signatures cut from correspondence," said John. This would explain Teesdale's pretensions to nobility. But I fancied that Milton was more than a client, and that John Marmaduke the younger had inherited his colourful personality from his great-grandfather, and that it was this creativity that had attracted Milton. Teesdale was twenty years older, but perhaps compared with the legitimate noblemen of Wentworth he was liberal in his attitude towards epileptics. Milton's nickname for him – Eel's Tail – was hardly reverential. Did he lead Milton astray?

THE HIGH LIFE

The kitchens in Wentworth Woodhouse, the Fitzwilliam family home, were a quarter of a mile from the dining room, further than in any other house in England. People used to joke that it took so long to get from the guest bedrooms to the breakfast room that if you left your room in the morning you might get there by lunchtime. The place was always overflowing with guests, despite the three hundred rooms. Lady Barbara Ricardo remembers two strangers being introduced to each other at the Doncaster races and discovering that they had both been staying at Wentworth throughout the previous week. It was that kind of house. Architectural experts like to make a point of how it was originally two houses back to back with no connecting doors. Quite some semi.

While few of Milton's descendants know about him, all of them know about his home. Wentworth came to the Fitzwilliams through the second Marquis of Rockingham, who died childless in 1772 and left the house, the grounds and various other estates – including 66,000 acres at Coollattin in Ireland – to his nephew, the fourth Earl Fitzwilliam, who himself owned an estate near Peterborough at Milton Park (from which the heir to the earldom derives his title). In this way 115,000 acres of Fitzwilliam empire were assembled. They made the family the twelfth-largest landowner in Britain and earned it a neat £60,000 a year in income. Not that this made the Fitzwilliams complacent. Quite the opposite. The fourth and fifth earls built coal mines, tar distilleries, iron foundries, a railway line and station with its own steam engine, and most of the houses in Wentworth village. By 1856 they were employing 869 miners.

The Fitzwilliams liked to have guests in the house and they liked to celebrate. When Milton's grandfather turned twenty-one in 1807, the family entertained a thousand people and this was what they consumed:

3 roasted oxen, 336 stone in weight
2 Scotch bullocks, 130 stone
26 roasted sheep, 177 stone 6 pounds
3 lambs
3 calves
10 hams
54 fowls
240 bushels of wheat

555 eggs
75 hogsheads of ale
6 hogsheads of small beer
473 bottles of good wine
23 gallons of rum
18 gallons of brandy
13 gallons of rum shrub

If you drove to Wentworth through the park and its conspiratorial herds of red deer and North American buffalo and long-horned cattle and Jacob sheep and you walked up the balustraded steps on the east side of the house and across the balcony behind the neo-classical columns and through the doors into the almost entirely marbled ballroom, you would be following the path not only of every Fitzwilliam but also of kings and queens, prime ministers and foreign secretaries, political luminaries and socialites and royalty of many nations, among them Gladstone and Edward VII, who was photographed on the balcony with Milton's father. There were special state rooms for such people. Wentworth Woodhouse has so many rooms you feel you are wandering around a village.

The best-known room, the one they all talked about, was designed by the fourth Earl to house the masterpiece his uncle had commissioned from George Stubbs in the 1760s: the immortalization of his beloved Arabian horse Whistlejacket. It is twelve feet high and the National Gallery took it in 1997 for just over £11 million, one great chestnut charger rearing out of the canvas and no background.

Charles Doyne says you hardly looked twice at the Whistle-jacket for the two other giant paintings in that drawing room and the elaborate screens and the twelve specially commissioned William IV giltwood armchairs. It was just another jewel among jewels. There were works of high art scattered all over the house. Giovanni Batista Foggini's huge sculpture *Samson and the Philistines*, now in the Victoria and Albert Museum; a portrait by Sir Anthony Van Dyck of the Countess of Carlisle, whose come-hither look they say bears out the theory that she was the Earl of Strafford's mistress; a portrait of William Shakespeare that used to belong to the seventeenth-century poet John Dryden; others by Reynolds, Raphael, Titian.

Wentworth has its own chapel, bakery and brewery, and cathedral-vault cellars that held tens of thousands of bottles of wine and 120-gallon casks of its own beer. It has a pillared soaking pond which drains the basement during flooding and has taken on mythic status as the Fitzwilliams' private fishing lake. What is fantasy and what is real regarding this house is clouded by history, for much has erroneously been assigned as myth on account of it appearing too outrageous to be true. Here is the truth as laid out by the *Illustrated London News* in September 1888:

> There are, it is to be feared, not many great country houses where the traditions of a generous past are kept up as they are at Wentworth. For six months in the year the great house is full of guests; at the rent-days in May and November three hundred guests a day feed in hall and kitchen for the best

part of a week; and ancient customs are kept up here, to be found, I believe, nowhere else in England. Some, indeed, have had to be discontinued, in deference to the growing sobriety of the age, or because of the neighbourhood of a great town like Sheffield. It is not so very long since, at the rent-day, all tenants were given as much beer as they could drink – and due provision of straw to "sleep it off" on; and every tramp who passed through the park had but to ask, and he was given a horn of ale and a crust of bread.

In spite of this high living, or because of it, the Fitzwilliams were held in great regard by the people who worked for them and tenanted their properties. This is because they concentrated as much on looking after those dependent on them as they did looking after themselves. The whole lives of the people living at Coollattin, Wentworth and Milton Park were bound up in the Fitzwilliam web of benevolent paternalism. Even today, every door in Wentworth village is painted Fitzwilliam green, and most of the paintings on the walls of the pubs are of Fitzwilliams hunting. Tradition and continuity counted for everything. The butcher who roasted the ox at Lord Peter's twenty-first birthday party was the same who had roasted the ox at his christening. If you played cricket well you could be sure of a better house.

People who knew the Fitzwilliams in the high days speak of them now as players in a set-piece drama with a pre-scripted ending, their history couched in tragic overtones. A family floored by calamity on calamity. They died too young and at all the wrong times. It started to come apart with the death of Billy in 1943, when they had to lease part of Wentworth and sell some of the contents to pay the death duties. Then Peter was killed five years later and it was fast downhill. Today they have neither Wentworth nor Coollattin. But the tragedy that people really dwell on is how the Fitzwilliams ran out of heirs. Because Peter had only a daughter, Lady Juliet, the title went to Eric, Milton's nephew. When he died four years later with no children it went to Tom, the son of Milton's first cousin George, the tenth and final Earl Fitzwilliam who lived at Milton Park. He died in 1979 with no male heirs and that was that. A state of affairs that would have seemed unlikely to the sixth Earl, father of eight sons and hot-blooded philanderers all of them.

Milton does not appear to have featured much in the family scene during his lifetime. Take his coming-of-age at Wentworth. The Fitzwilliams were famous for their extravagant parties. On February 11, 1911, for example, Billy celebrated his son's christening with several thousand guests and onlookers, a roast ox and what the *Rotherham Advertiser* called "the biggest private display of fireworks for five years," including "thousands upon thousands of bombs, stars and rockets," a firelight portrait of the earl and his wife and, in the provocative spirit of the age, "a set piece in which a British Dreadnought will bombard and beat in a most realistic fashion the Dreadnought of a 'Continental Power.'" Milton's coming-of-age party on July 27, 1860, was different.

For a start, according to the local newspaper reports, he was not there for it. Neither was his family: most of them were abroad. It was celebrated instead by 180 of his father's tenants, who drank toasts to the young Lord with the ale that had been maturing since his christening day while the masons and carpenters played a cricket match on the lawn.

How does a person feel when his family does not find it appropriate to mark his rite of passage into adulthood by attending it? He was hardly going to turn up alone. I was beginning to feel a considerable sympathy for him, and rather a distaste for his family. Not showing up at his party felt at best like an exhibition of disinterest, at worst of disapproval. Perhaps they considered him unworthy to be heir, on account of his illness or his behaviour. Doubtless they had the family name to consider.

As the eldest son, Milton had a great deal to live up to with his father such a powerful figure and so popular, ADC to Queen Victoria and all that. Fitzwilliam men in those days were notorious above all for two things. The first was immoderate sexual behaviour. Rumour has it that Milton's father used to point at a painting of a fox hunt commissioned for his golden wedding anniversary and boast that he had bred every living thing in it. Aside from himself, two of his daughters, five horses and a pack of hounds, it depicts a huntsman and a member of the hunt staff. Milton's youngest brother, Reginald, made one of the maids at Wentworth pregnant. Their mother when she heard this remarked: "Thank God, I was beginning to think he wasn't entire." The maid was given a farm and instructed to choose a husband from among the footmen, the usual procedure in such cases. Reginald went to New Zealand – to shoot emus. Stories of illegitimate Fitzwilliam sons and daughters abound in the pubs around Wentworth. Philandering, you could say, was in the blood. And reading between the lines of *The North-West Passage by Land*, it appears that Milton inherited it too.

The other persistent Fitzwilliam tradition was politics. The Fitzwilliams extended the paternalistic government of their estates to wider society, for the politics of their estates were simply the manifestation of solid Whig principles. The estate was a microcosm of the national stage. The family was a mainstay of Whiggism in parliament, Rockingham as prime minister in the 1760s, the fourth Earl as a friend of Charles James Fox, the fifth for his campaigning on the Irish Poor Laws, the sixth as a friend of Gladstone, despite disagreeing with him over Irish Home Rule in 1886 (Fitzwilliam remaining a Unionist).

Milton himself would win two elections for the Whigs in the Southern Division of the West Riding of Yorkshire, in 1865 and 1868, "gallantly" in the first case, reported one newspaper, since "other Liberal candidates were sought in vain." But he was not considered an orator and never excelled where his father and grandfather had. How much of a disappointment must that have been to his father and how much to him? What was expected was not what was destined, and this Milton would have seen laid out plain in Gladstone's answer to his request for ministerial office in 1868: "I am sorry to say that on a full review of the various elements of

Wentworth Woodhouse in Yorkshire, the Fitzwilliam family
home up to the 1980s

Milton's father, the sixth
Earl Fitzwilliam

Milton's mother,
the Countess

An unlikely alliance:
Milton's party after
crossing the Rockies,
September 1863.
(Left to right) the
Assiniboine's wife,
the Assiniboine,
Cheadle, Milton
(with headband), the
Assiniboine's son

Milton in his late twenties as an MP

Laura, Milton's wife, with their first daughter, Laura

A model Englishman? Milton in Wentworth Woodhouse

Laura, Milton's first-born

Mabel, Milton's second child

Theresa, Milton's youngest and my great-grandmother,
on her engagement

Billy, Milton's son
and heir, who was
born in Canada

Billy (centre) receives a cup from representatives of
the miners at the christening of his son Peter,
Wentworth Woodhouse, February 11, 1911.

Grandma (left)
and Aunt Chris, in
England before the
Second World War

Aunt Chris (left) and Grandma in 1970

age, experience, former service, and of the numerous comparative questions which must be taken into account I find myself unable to ask you to become a member of the government. It is with very sincere regret that I announce this conclusion." I guessed that of the "numerous comparative questions" that had to be taken into account the most pressing was his epilepsy, which in four years would in any case take him out of politics forever. After all, it was not usual and would be a little embarrassing to have a minister convulsing on the floor of the House of Commons.

Not that any of this appears to have undermined his belief in his own political destiny. The voters of Yorkshire got a hatful of it when he contested his seat for the second time:

> Gentlemen, electors and non-electors,
> When I came before you on a former occasion I told you that I was young and inexperienced and that I had few definite opinions, but I am now enabled to say to you that my views on most of the important topics of the day are firmly fixed. . . . I believe that the united forces of the free and liberal people of this constituency will again carry our colours to the front and will ensure, to the great and glorious principles which we profess, a sure and undoubted victory.

His enthusiasm and confidence even prompted his mother to warn him of the perils of extravagant ambition. She advised him against moving a resolution in the House of Commons before he was ready:

If you begin *too* soon either to speak or to act . . . you will destroy your chance of future influence for good. The Bible maxim of being "swift to hear, slow to speak," is the right one. You know my dearest William that one of the greatest gratifications I could have would be to see you useful to your fellow creatures in public as well as in private. But a desire for personal distinction may I fear hurry you on too much.

When the voters of West Riding elected him he fought for their interests, in characteristic mechanical detail. His contributions to the House of Commons were never in danger of stirring the national consciousness and they were notable mostly for their pedanticisms, though some of them were at least relevant to his constituency, or to a few members of it. But by a long way Milton's most significant contribution to the House in numbers of questions asked and time on his feet and general colour and controversy was over the future of Britain's dominions in Canada.

He was tickled more by Canada than by anything Yorkshire could throw up. He was especially keen to discuss the Red River Settlement – founded by a relative of his mother, the fifth Earl of Selkirk – and the unsettled prairies and the San Juan Islands off British Columbia which the Americans were preparing to hive off (the political implications of that would be the subject of Milton's second book). Over Canada he got steamed up and came into his combative and erratic own. Often when denied a satisfactory answer he would repeat the same question on consecutive days, and several times in a month. The Attorney General once accused Milton of putting to him "about the longest question that had ever been addressed by one Member of Parliament to another." Another member, befuddled by Milton's persistence over trade licences, declared: "The noble Lord's questions are not always very easy to answer, and not always easy to understand."

You need some talent to get yourself elected to the House of Commons but Milton's did not lie in intelligibility. He was not fond of punctuation (nor of spelling) and the fewer sentences the better. In the notes to one of his travel lectures most of the sentences are more than 150 words long. Some are more than 250 words long. One hopes he didn't read them verbatim. It was as if he didn't have time in life for the nuances of grammar. The words just seemed to tumble out. The editors of *The North-West Passage by Land* must have had their work cut out.

Arguing with Milton cannot have been enjoyable. He was a pedant on the points that mattered to him. He once threatened legal action in a dispute with the 1st West York Yeomanry Cavalry, of which he was an officer, over an unpaid dinner bill. He proofread his books with the attention of a subeditor, picking out the most trivial slips in typography and punctuation. He also worried how other people saw him. He insisted on removing from the final version of *The North-West Passage by Land* two passages that cast him as ungallant. The first was at Niagara Falls when he and Cheadle entered a room unshaven and dressed down, and unwittingly cleared it of its female occupants.

The second was when Cheadle returned to their winter hut in the woods north of the Saskatchewan River to find him cooking, an image Milton reckoned did not fit him, and so wrote to his companion to put him right: "I met you about a quarter of a mile from the hut on my way to our place to look for you anyhow I never did any cooking there for the woman did that always."

I found other examples of Milton's almost obsessive attention to detail. He had a remarkable knowledge of Church history, and would write long letters to *The Times* deliberating the slightest points of Ecclesiastical doctrine, though he considered them anything but slight. His most famous exchange was over the alterations made by Parliament and the Convocation of the Church of England to the *Book of Common Prayer* in 1661, and in particular over where the holy table should stand in a church, a matter that he succeeded in dragging out over a full eighty-nine lines in London's major newspaper. With this inclination, you can see why Milton might have made a genius mechanic.

He may have been fastidious but this does not appear to have prevented him enjoying himself. He seems to have been happiest on a horse. A letter of recommendation from a friend to a gentlemen's club in New York describes him in a passage about his riding abilities as "an extremely gifted sportsman." His passion and the passion of every Fitzwilliam, what they seemed to live for more than any-thing, was hunting. If they weren't hunting foxes at Wentworth then they would be hunting them at Coollattin. Milton's father sometimes hunted six days a week, and if he was hunting at Wentworth on Friday then he would have to finish early to take the train to Coollattin so he could hunt there on Saturday. Lady Fitzwilliam used to complain that he had only two interests in life, and hunting was one of them.

Milton shared one other Fitzwilliam disposition: death before forty. An alarming number of Fitzwilliams and their progeny have died young, several of them in riding accidents. Milton, like his father's elder brother, would die – aged thirty-seven – two decades before his father, who like the woeful patriarch of some Russian tragedy lost five of his children in his lifetime.

He shared these things with his family and he went to Eton College and Trinity College, Cambridge, like the rest of them. But he clearly didn't fit in, or his family didn't let him. He seemed to confide more in friends, and he chose a colourful bunch, most of them older than himself: Cheadle, Teesdale, and the Liberal peer Lord Houghton, known as the "only poet" in the Upper House and for securing the laureateship for Lord Tennyson. Houghton was thirty years older than Milton, yet he wrote Milton's obituary for the Royal Geographical Society archives. Houghton is described in Chambers's *Encyclopaedia* of 1895 as:

A traveller, a philanthropist, an unrivalled after-dinner speaker, and Rogers' successor in the art of breakfast-giving. He went up in a balloon, and down in a diving-bell; he was the first publishing Englishman who gained access to the harems of the East; he championed oppressed nationalities, liberty of conscience, fugitive slaves, and the rights of women; he counted among his friends Hallam, Tennyson, Thackeray, Dickens, Carlyle, Sydney Smith, Landor, Cardinal Wiseman, Heine, Thirlwall, and a host of others.

He sounded Milton's type. They corresponded frequently: about twin-screw yachts and water pumps and other engineering matters, the need to find Milton's brother-in-law a seat in Parliament, reviewers who might be sympathetic towards *The North-West Passage by Land.* The things about which a son might ask his father.

My great-great-grandfather is a mysterious figure but my great-great-grandmother is more so. Pretty much the only thing anyone knows about her is that she married Milton. There are a couple of letters and telegrams from her in my grandmother's brown suitcase, but most of what I learnt I picked up – inevitably – from newspapers.

Laura Maria Theresa Beauclerk was daughter of the late Lord Charles Beauclerk (son of the eighth Duke of St. Albans), who was killed trying to rescue the crew of a lifeboat off Scarborough in 1861. She and Milton were married on a sunny morning in August 1867 at St. George's, Hanover Square, London, with a ring cut by him from a gold nugget he had sieved four years earlier from the Upper Fraser River at Cariboo, British Columbia. She was eighteen, ten years younger than him. In photographs she looks more like fourteen, rather nervous and rather serious, though Milton looks serious too. I wondered whether on that day she had any idea what kind of family she was marrying into, and that she and Milton would be spending most of the rest of their lives in semi-isolation, protected from embarrassment, guilt, stigma and expectation several thousand miles west of anywhere she'd been before. Within five years of their wedding Milton and she were living in exile – according to one account under an assumed name – in the United States.

How often do the hurt and vulnerable find each other. Laura Milton suffered from a chronic kidney disease and she may have suffered other things for she was ill, it seems, as regularly as her husband. Frequently they could not keep appointments because Lady Milton was "not in a sufficiently strong state to travel," or "abroad on account of her health." Their family doctor reported in 1873 that "her health is still very indifferent and she is quite a cripple yet. Lord Milton is not so well." It's a wonder they managed anything together in their ten years of marriage, let alone produce four children. After Milton died the children spent a lot of their time at Wentworth while Laura stayed in the United States at their house in Richmond, Virginia, for long periods too ill to move. She wrote to my great-grandmother a year and a half before her death: "My darling little woman, I should have written to you long ago to wish you very many happy returns of your birthday but Mother has been ill for a long time and is only now able to write to you."

Laura died, on holiday in Torquay, on March 20, 1886, from a urinary infection, nine years after Milton and at precisely the same age. For him she was a partner in suffering. Did his family sanction the marriage? Most of them were at the wedding. Perhaps they had little choice, now that he was twenty-eight and an MP. Or perhaps it was somehow more acceptable because she also was ill.

☼

Milton's life sounds tragic when you read the bare statistics. In reality it was heroic. For rather than stay and suffer his illness and the suffocating social position into which he had been born, he went out and found a better life. He transcended the hardest of psychological barriers: that to which he was accustomed. It can be difficult to leave what you know, however badly it is hurting you. He was only twenty-two when he began his Canadian journey.

That time he did not make a clean break. When he returned, aged twenty-four, he appears to have done his best to fit the role laid out for him at birth: he lived at Wentworth and became a Member of Parliament. But despite his partial success at this he was attempting steps in off-sized shoes: an epileptic in search of accommodation where none existed. Sometimes in photographs from this period, when he was between twenty-five and thirty-two, he looks like his father, with sideburns and a shot at an "I run the show" pose. At other times he looks washed out with troubled eyes. The only photograph in which he looks truly his own man, hostage neither to his father nor to any life other than his own, was taken when he was twenty-four in San Francisco and he'd come half-starved off the Rockies after a year and a half in wilderness of his own choosing. Yet he would make concessions to his upbringing in his book. The Empire-building stuff was straight out of the Fitzwilliam doctrine of imperialism. He would be well into his thirties before he could leave all that forever.

I had a strong idea of what Milton was like: proud and ambitious, on account of his politics; flamboyant, on account of his friends; pedantic, a little obsessively so; mechanically gifted; a fine horseman; ill-treated; and for what he did to overcome that, courageous. Out of curiosity, and because I had so little material to go on, I commissioned an expert to analyze his handwriting. Such studies of character can be remarkably accurate. The portrait she drew of Milton agreed in many ways with mine, but it was even more impressive. She described him as emotionally highly-strung, and bound to react with considerable mood swings. She referred to his "striving for excellence, his drive, his mental agility and his intellectual curiosity." She said he "did not like to feel confined by too much narrow conventionality." But she did not pick up any pointers to his epilepsy. Did he transcend this as well?

Milton left for Canada with Dr. Cheadle a few months after breaking off his engagement to Dorcas Chichester. *The North-West Passage by Land* has an imperialist edge to it and gives the impression the authors went out as servants of the Crown in all but name, but it seems clear he was escaping. Why Canada? He could not have chosen a more masculine place at that time, nor a more liberal one. He also had connections there: the legacy of his kinsman, Lord Selkirk, at the Red River Settlement. The ninth Earl of Southesk, a friend of his father's, had crossed the prairies in 1859. Milton himself had been on a hunting trip to Canada in 1860. Being a Fitzwilliam had its advantages. Whatever the reason, it was the making of him. He found a Wild West frontier and a raw-earth hardship to tough out, men to ride with who did not query his past or future, the only pressure the need to feed himself and wrap out the cold, read the stars for the next day's miles, survive the night and the swollen rivers and the punctiliousness of his best friend, for here was his true liberation.

A NEW WORLD

They sailed from Liverpool on June 19, 1862, Milton and Cheadle and a whole host of colourful characters destined for outlandish adventure. They shared their table each evening with a Canadian colonel, "dignified, majestic, and speaking as with authority," who "discoursed political wisdom to an admiring and obsequious audience" – until, that is, he became seasick.

The purser, a jolly Irishman, came up at the moment and cried, "Holloa, colonel! Glad to see you all right again." "All right, sir!" cried the colonel, fiercely; "all right, sir? I'm *not* all right. I'm *frightfully ill*, sir! I've suffered the tortures of the condemned; horrible beyond expression; but it's not the pain I complain of; that, sir, a soldier like myself knows how to endure. But I'm thoroughly ashamed of myself, and shall never hold up my head again!"

They befriended two Roman Catholic bishops who were on their way back from a meeting with the Pope in Rome, one of them tall and emaciated and the very picture of an ascetic, the other "a round, fat, oily man of God" with a weakness for food and tobacco; and as an antidote to them, an old lady afflicted with "Papophobia," who spent the crossing condemning the Queen for her weakness in accepting a sideboard as a present from Pius IX. Soon after embarking in Canada they made the acquaintance of Captain Hutchinson:

> Or, more properly speaking, he had made ours. The gallant captain was rather extensively got up, his face smooth shaven, with the exception of the upper lip, which was graced with a light, silky moustache. He wore a white hat, cocked knowingly on one side, and sported an elegant walking cane; the blandest of smiles perpetually beamed on his countenance, and he accosted us in the most affable and insinuating manner, with some remark about the heat of the weather. Dextrously improving the opening thus made, he placed himself in a few minutes on the most intimate terms.

The gathering of such characters is more believable if you consider what was going on in North America at that time and consider too the people who were drawn to it. It was the second year of the American Civil War and the

Confederates had just defeated the Union forces at Fredericksburg. Gold had been found in the Thompson and Fraser rivers in British Columbia and that place declared the new El Dorado. The government was pushing Canada – today's Quebec and Ontario – as the new promised land, enticing farmers from Europe and America with promises of free land and fertile soil (and no notice of deep-freeze winters and insect plagues). Buffalo still lived in the wild unsettled country west of the Great Lakes, drawing big-game hunters from England and America for what they considered the best sport anywhere. All this pulled in a cast of unlikely candidates, bit-part players of the game who were wedded to no rule book: soldiers, gold-seekers, hunters, fur-traders, Empire-builders, missionaries, explorers, Yankee-haters, Indian-haters, the gullible and the optimistic, most of them young and most of them men. While Milton was in Toronto, a travelling "Hippozoonomadon" show reached town. It featured a hippopotamus from the White Nile "of which Job says 'Upon the Earth there is not his like.'" It was not a conventional world, and there was room enough for anything the human race could throw up.

Whether or not Milton knew what he was getting into, it was brought home to him soon enough. He and Cheadle visited Niagara Falls and travelled by railway through Detroit and Chicago to La Crosse on the banks of the Mississippi and then by steamer up the river to St. Paul, west on the nascent Great Pacific Railroad to St. Anthony, and by stagecoach to Georgetown in Minnesota on the Red River. They met many people in this area, which was fairly well settled, and stayed with several of them. At one house they befriended their host's mongrel terrier, Rover, and rather heartlessly persuaded him to sell it, despite the anguished wailings of his wife and sister for whom this dog seemed to represent their single link with their old life. A fortnight after their visit, these people – indeed almost all the whites in that part of Minnesota – were killed by Sioux Indians.

Most Europeans at that time were patronizing and racist about North American Indians. It was the spirit of the age. Milton held different views. He was clearly fascinated by them. When later that year he came to depend on them, and even fell in love with one, he became a true sympathizer. He would become fluent in Cree, an accomplishment of which few non-Indians could boast. Perhaps he felt an empathy with their suffering at the hands of the Establishment. This is his reaction after seeing an Indian for the first time:

He was leaning against a tree, smoking his pipe with great dignity, not deigning to move or betray the slightest inter-est as the train went past him. We could not help reflecting – as, perhaps, he was doing – with something of sadness upon the changes which had taken place since his ancestors were lords of the soil. . . . We could well imagine the disgust of these sons of silence and stealth at the noisy trains which rush through the forests, and the steamers which dart along lakes and rivers, once the favourite haunt of game, now driven far away. How bitterly in their hearts they must curse that steady, unfaltering, inevitable advance of the great army of whites, recruited from every corner of the earth, spreading over the land like locusts – too strong to resist, too cruel and unscrupulous to mingle with them in peace and friendship!

This was magnanimous compared with the views of other writers of that era, whose fantasies helped shape many enduring prejudices about North American Indians. Take, for example, Robert Ballantyne, who worked for the Hudson's Bay Company in Canada during the 1840s:

> When starving, the Indian will not hesitate to appease the cravings of hunger by resorting to cannibalism; and there were some old dames with whom I was myself acquainted, who had at different periods eaten several of their children. Indeed, some of them, it was said, had also eaten their husbands. (*Hudson's Bay*, Robert Ballantyne, 1848)

Although the Sioux around Georgetown were already on the warpath when Milton and Cheadle passed through, in the fashion of British adventurers they balked at this threat of violence, branded cowards those who didn't, and set off up the Red River to Fort Garry and the Red River Settlement in canoes against the advice of everyone they met. They arrived two weeks later suffering only sunburn and mosquito bites.

I arrived in Canada in February with the rivers still frozen and I had never known such cold. The cold was the first thing that got to me. The second thing was the way people behaved. Meeting strangers in Canada is a different thing to meeting strangers in England. Strangers in Canada behave as if you are already their friend. An English person unused to such openness might treat it as pathological: what instability are they harbouring that makes them so friendly? But you would have to be pathologically English not to warm to it. There were eight Canadians on my bus from Ottawa airport to the centre of town and at the end of the ride I had the names and addresses of each of them, their political allegiances, opinions on the city, genealogy and plans for the new millennium. Within days I had collected several dozen addresses. I think they liked Milton's story. He was one of the original Canadian pioneers, and for me to be following him was a grand thing as far as they were concerned.

I didn't wait around in Ottawa as I wanted to get to Winnipeg. Winnipeg, where the West begins, is where Milton got on his horse. It is built on the site of Selkirk's Red River Settlement and Fort Garry at the junction of the Red and Assiniboine rivers. On my first day in the city the wind came off the prairies and down Main Street and Portage Avenue and any street that ran westwards to the slightest degree and it felt like a wind that had blown a great distance unhindered. Wind of awesome and primeval quality.

At Fort Garry Milton met up with his friend Louis La Ronde, a French-Indian Métis (in Milton's politically incorrect parlance, a "halfbreed"). La Ronde had been

Milton's guide two years earlier when he had come out to hunt buffalo with the Métis west of the Red River. The two had rather hit it off: "[La Ronde] indulged in the most extravagant demonstrations of delight at seeing him again, and expressed his readiness to go with him to the end of the world, if required."

In the early 1850s, La Ronde had accompanied Dr. John Rae on his search for Franklin, who had been missing since setting out to find a northwest passage by sea though the Canadian Arctic in 1845. Now he would go with Milton to try to stop him getting lost. La Ronde had a reputation as a great hunter and trapper. This, Milton noted, was not the only thing for which he had a reputation: "He was a fine, tall, well-built fellow, with a handsome face and figure, and was reported to be quite irresistible amongst the fair sex." A genealogist I later met in Saskatoon, who keeps extensive records on Indian families, told me he had turned up seven Louis La Rondes from that era, each associated with a different woman, and he is fairly certain that most of them were the same man: Milton's Louis.

Fort Garry would be Milton's and Cheadle's last brush with civilization for some time. They stocked up: three hundredweight of flour per person, one hundredweight of pemmican (a cement-blend of dried meat, animal fat and berries), 20 pounds of tobacco, 22 pounds of gunpowder, 56 pounds of shot, 20 pounds of tea, 10 pounds of coffee, 14 pounds of salt, 3 pounds of pepper, a blanket, a buffalo robe, one pair of beaverteen trousers, a revolver, a hunting knife and 8 gallons of rum. In appearance, at least, they went

Native, discarding their English boots and coats for moccasins and Caribou-skin shirts. They acquired horses: Milton a favourite of his from before, Big Red, "the hero of a thousand runs"; Cheadle a curious-looking brute called Bucephalus, which insisted on stopping at every gate and fence in expectation of being tied up, a trait they put down to "the gossipping habits of his previous owner."

Milton would ride a horse all two thousand miles from Fort Garry to the Pacific. This for me was going to be rather a challenge, especially as it was still winter. Milton learnt to ride when he learnt to walk. So I compromised, electing to walk or hitchhike for the first part of the journey across Manitoba, Saskatchewan and Alberta and find a horse when I got to the Rockies. This meant I would have to leave out the buffalo robes and the beaverteen trousers. I allowed myself one luxury item: a cricket ball. I like cricket very much. People I know who don't play cricket, which includes all the Canadians I have met, find the sport incomprehensible. I agree it can be an exacting game, one for pedants even. I don't know whether Milton played it, though they had a cricket pitch in front of Wentworth Woodhouse, and an ancestor of Laura, the Rev. Lord Frederick Beauclerk, played for England and was described in his time as "the greatest of all cricketers." I hoped for some of that blood through my veins.

A ROAD LESS TRAVELLED

In the middle of March I took a bus from Winnipeg to the edge of the plains beyond Portage la Prairie. It had been snowing for two days. I followed a small road south from where the bus dropped me towards the Assiniboine River and it was long and straight like all roads across the prairie which cover the land as a grid. Somewhere off this road I hoped to pick up the old Carlton Trail, or what was left of it. Whether or not this trail still existed on the ground it would exist forever in the consciousness of this country for it helped to give birth to it. It is an old Indian trail and an artery through the wilderness followed by Milton to the Rocky Mountains and every other nineteenth-century explorer and fur-trader and the first two generations of settlers. Today, some of the trail crosses farmland and some of it follows roads and railway lines. Some of it is still visible and bears the old cart-ruts and some of it is lost forever.

Everyone had advised against hitchhiking. There had been some nasty incidents, they said; people had lost their cars to hitchhikers and now no one would risk charity for a stranger. Perhaps they'd risk it for an Englishman. In anticipation of the scarcity of traffic I had sewn a Union Jack onto the front of my rucksack. In other countries this would have considerably reduced my chances. In Canada people seemed to make a point of stopping for it, if only to ask about the health of the Queen.

In the first three hours on this road I was passed by a car, a tractor and a bus full of schoolchildren, who found it rather amusing that their driver didn't stop. I resisted exchanging my thumb for a finger. An uncharitable sentiment perhaps, but it was a low and empty moment. I had given up my job for this. I was going to miss an entire cricket season. I had left behind my long-suffering girlfriend. Four years together and then, aged thirty, off I go in search of a dead person. "What am I to make of it?" she wondered, with good cause. She was the most patient person I knew and she never tried to stop me, but no one could be this patient for long. There was going to be trouble. Was this my Incredible Journey or was it my Great Escape? Such thoughts rendered heavier by a long and lonely road, and by a busload of cavorting schoolchildren. Then along came Steve.

Steve in his wildest dreams is a rodeo king. In reality he does well to last five seconds on an upstart steer before hitting the dirt. This doesn't bother him. Like thousands of others in Canada's cowboy country he lives for the ring in summer and dreams of it in winter, the slamming open of the pen gates and the hush of the crowd, wild animal-shudder through untamed flesh. "I've done drugs and drunk alcohol and there ain't no high like riding one-handed on a buckin' cow." He has been around horses all his life and breaks them in for a living. When he sits on a chair he approaches it from the side and swings his leg over the back. His wife, Moe, says he spurs in bed sometimes when he's dreaming. Kyle, his fourteen-year-old son, has started riding rodeos as well, losing his Stetson with the best of them in the dust and dancing hooves. Moe gets criticized by other mothers for letting him do this but it's in his blood and you can't stop them when they're born with it and no one should try. They showed me their first rides on video and then we watched a video of a rodeo championship in Houston, and both tapes were breaking up from over-watching.

Steve is lean and fit-looking, he is not heavy and I can imagine him playing the rodeo part. He says he is built for the active life. This means the country life. He and Moe live off the land as far as anyone can: they keep pigs, chickens and rabbits for food or trade and hunt birds, deer and elk and gather Saskatoon berries or blueberries in summer for jelly or pie. In this way they feed a family of seven, with occasional forays into supermarkets for Coca-Cola and hot dogs. Steve knows the name of every tree, bird, flower and animal in these parts, knows their habits and what of them he can eat and what he cannot and he can tell the age of a deer from a hundred yards. He told me a thing or two about walking in a Canadian winter and he told me things about the country-side a book could never tell you: how to track an animal on dry earth, how to eat a porcupine without feeling sick. He said that was how you learned around here. Have people tell you. He said that was how Milton would have learned.

Steve and Kyle picked me up in their rusting white Ford estate wagon when I still had three miles to the river and they took me the rest of the way. The ice which was several feet deep in places had started to melt in puddles on the surface and the ice in some of the creeks off the river had melted right through, and the water was flooding the plain. It was a treacherous place to walk alone at this time of year, Steve said. A man could die in a freezing creek and no one would ever know.

They took me to their house back up the road from the river and they brought out maps of the area from the days before it was settled, Steve and Moe and Kyle and four young daughters crowding round as if for some exhaustive treasure hunt. Out loud and with great ceremony, Steve read the passage in my copy of Cheadle's diary that describes the party's passing: "Dined off pemmican with Worcester sauce and then moved on two miles to another swamp . . . through undulating prairie and scrubs . . . forward some 10 miles to a very pretty lake, up some height and surrounded by trees, a very jolly camping ground . . . retire, after mushroom supper."

There followed nodding of the judicious, all heads con-comitant. Then Steve said: "Well, you don't want to be going anywhere near that river then."

"Because of the swamps," I suggested.

"No, because the trail didn't go anywhere near there." More thoughtful nodding from the committee. They reckoned from Cheadle's diary entry and from what they knew of the area that the Carlton Trail had never reached the river but had passed north of their house to Jackson's Lake, the only piece of water in the area and the only rise in any direction for miles. It was an inauspicious start. How many heroic explorers got lost on their first day?

I camped under a maple tree in Steve's garden and the next day I walked north for a mile and then west as directed by him and his family down a dirt track towards Jackson's Lake, and the air was above freezing and there was heat in the sun and the landscape was very still. Every movement or sign of movement at this time is a revelation of spring. White-tailed deer with tails snapping up like semaphore flags trumpeted out of the stillness and their prints were there in the mud. The track turned north to the lake where my great-great-grandfather had camped after a mushroom supper one hundred and thirty-six years, six months and twenty days before me.

Was it the same lake, the same jolly camping ground? Geographically, perhaps, but Milton would hardly recognize them. One hundred and thirty years is a long time in the life of the land. Entire lakes can disappear and new ones emerge, generations of trees rise from the soil and return to it, hillocks erode to level ground. Even mountains move. Between Milton's visit to Niagara Falls and mine the face of the falls had eroded a hundred metres or so back up the river. These were the same falls and not the same; Jackson's Lake a reincarnation in a string of lakes reborn at the same latitude and longitude. How relevant is it to retrace someone's footsteps through a landscape they would barely recognize? The prairies have been shaped to the needs of humankind as much as any land anywhere: grasslands and swamps framed into fields, every square mile of chaos fenced and held to account by map and deed. Where Milton rode through "rich, park-like country, swarming with wildfowl" or "bare rolling prairie, destitute of tree or shrub," I was confined to tracks or roads between fields, an approximation of the old trail. A different age, different mission. Such journeys as this in the shadow of others are traced in the mind as much as on the earth. A pilgrimage has little to do with the getting there.

The next morning I burnt holes in my socks trying to dry them on my fire. More incompetence of a greenhorn traveller. I was pleased to discover later that Milton and Cheadle had done exactly the same thing a few miles up the trail. This inaugurated what Cheadle in his diary called "a most unlucky day." He lost the top of the shot bag Milton had lent him. He missed five ducks in succession and fired three barrels at snipe without troubling them, an unprecedented lapse in accuracy. Later he gave chase to a badger:

> I get within 30 yards and give him a charge of No. 3; it turns him over and he stops and grins at me; other barrel not loaded from losing shot bag. I run after him and turn him repeatedly, trying to cram in a charge of buck shot in gun.

Voudrie [a Métis hunter they had hired] comes up and hits him over nose with switch, but he succeeds in getting to earth to my chagrin.

Although publishing firms in the 1860s did not have to pander to an animal-rights lobby, Cassell, Petter and Galpin thought better of including the badger-baiting in *The North-West Passage by Land*. However, other dubious sporting achievements are celebrated with no detail spared. On one level the book is no more than an account of a rollicking hunting expedition. Milton and Cheadle found game everywhere and shot it whenever possible: pheasants, duck of several species, geese, swans, snipe, prairie grouse, eagles, elk, antelope, wolf, skunk, badger, bear and buffalo. They did not seem to mind whether the quarry was sporting or whether it was strictly game:

> The young geese, although almost full-grown and feathered, were not yet able to fly, but afforded capital sport. When hotly pursued they dived as we came near in the canoes, and, if too hardly pushed, took to the shore. This was generally a fatal mistake; Milton immediately landed with Rover, who quickly discovered them lying with merely their heads hidden in the grass or bushes, and they were then captured.

They found that the most successful way to knock off prairie grouse in the spring was to approach them at dawn or dusk when they gathered in large groups for a mating dance: "A prairie chicken dance is a most ludicrous sight, and whilst they are engaged in it, they become so absorbed in the performance that it is easy to approach them. We took advantage of their weakness for a social hop, and broke up the ball in a most sanguinary manner." This method, they assured their readers, was used only when starvation beckoned. Every victim was dispatched in the name of Britain abroad so perhaps their readers applauded it.

Milton in the book offers hints to future sportsmen, as if to persuade people that proper hunting was as essential to the future of British North America as proper politics. A rifle, he advises, though effective against larger game, is useless against the feathered variety and should never be taken as an only weapon. Since a traveller could not hope to carry two guns through the roughest terrain he should consider leaving the rifle at home and settling on a double-barrelled smooth-bore shotgun, which will shoot various sizes of shot as well as a single ball. I felt ill-equipped: my most potent weapon was a penknife.

I had found one of the shotguns used by Milton in the storage rooms of the Canadian Museum of Civilization in Ottawa. It was a Westley Richards, double-barrelled, cap-and-ball 14-gauge with a beautifully polished stock and Damascus steel barrels and a ramrod under the barrels. It had been left to the museum with a clutch of other relics from the expedition by one of Cheadle's sons in 1935. I lifted it to my shoulder and rested my cheek on the smooth stock and imagined scattering a group of duck on the Assiniboine at dusk, hammers slamming down on mercury caps and the blast of the powder and the kick of the shot. The museum also has one of the explorers' Colt brevet muzzle-loading 36-calibre cap-and-ball revolvers with steel and brass barrel and an engraving of a horseback hunt on the chamber, though as the museum's firearms expert pointed out, such a weapon was fairly inaccurate and useless in a hunt and would have been carried by Milton and Cheadle for self-defence, or to shoot a bolting horse if the rider got jammed in the stirrup. I could have done with one. It would have made hitchhiking more entertaining.

In Milton's day, the prairies of what are now Manitoba and Saskatchewan were littered with buffalo skulls. Of all the game Milton pursued, this was the animal he and every hunter prized most. It was also the animal the Indians of the plains relied on for food. By the 1860s buffalo were becoming scarce in North America and Indians were starving. There were not enough to satisfy the hunger of Indians and the blood lust of Europeans. Many Indians resented the colonials killing for sport what they killed to survive. In *The North-West Passage by Land*, Milton relates a conversation with a Cree chief concerned about the advance of the white man. The Cree notes that Milton and Cheadle are clearly great chiefs in their own country, well supplied with blankets, tea, tobacco, rum and splendid guns. But there is one thing they lack – buffalo. He himself does not have great riches. The only thing he does have is buffalo. Why then should they visit his country to destroy the one good thing he has, simply for their own pleasure? It is a difficult argument to refute and Milton doesn't try.

A letter from Alexander Morris, Lieutenant-Governor of Manitoba and the North-West Territories from 1872 to 1877, to the Minister of the Interior in Ottawa mentions that a band of Indians held Milton prisoner for several days to prevent him chasing a herd of buffalo hundreds of miles away from their camp. Cheadle does not mention this incident in his journal and neither does Milton in the book, although it could have taken place when he came out two years before for the Great Fall Hunt, or when he returned later with his family in the summer of 1872. Morris correctly predicted to within a couple of years (early 1880s) the extinction of the wild buffalo at the hands of Indians and whites in Canada, noting that in 1872 traders had shipped out of the country over 50,000 buffalo robes, and C$100,000 in other furs.

To hunt a buffalo the favoured course was to ride at the herd at full tilt across the prairie and separate out from the running and panicking animals a single bull or cow and then pursue this, turning it as a hunting dog courses a hare until you could bring the horse level with the buffalo and fire your shotgun into its heart. It was a dangerous sport, for the prairie was full of holes deep enough to trip a galloping horse and an injured buffalo could turn on its tormentor. "It was magnificent and it was war," was how one writer of that era described it.

The anticipation of the hunt gave Milton as much thrill

as the chase: " 'Les Boeufs, les boeufs, les boeufs sont proches!' Girths were tightened, and guns examined, and then we went forward at a foot's pace, feeling in much the same nervous condition as a freshman at the university in his first boat-race, waiting for the sound of the gun which gives the signal to start." And finally: " 'Hurrah! hurrah! allez!' and away we all went, helter-skelter, arms brandishing, and heels hammering our horses' ribs in true half-breed fashion – a mad, wild charge."

For the four hundred miles from Fort Garry to Fort Carlton, on the North Saskatchewan River north of present-day Saskatoon, Milton and Cheadle were accompanied by Charles Alston Messiter, disguised in anagram as "Treemiss" in *The North-West Passage by Land*. He had sailed from Liverpool with them and his sole purpose in visiting Canada was to hunt big game. His book, not published until 1890, was entitled *Sport and Adventures among the North-American Indians*, though from reading it you get the impression that Indians were an inconvenience and rather got in the way of the sport. Messiter concluded after his first meeting with the Cree that "they were much better when not seen too near." He managed to fall out with most of the Indians he came across, as illustrated by the captions to the pictures in his book: "He stopped about six feet from me and shook his fist"; "I drew my revolver and fired at him"; "I fired at his chest"; "The Comanches made a rush at us." He had even brought from England an Indian-hating bloodhound that had to be tied up and restrained when any were in camp.

He also fell out with Milton. According to Cheadle the

two of them argued incessantly. They disagreed over everything from North American politics to which of them had fired the shot that felled a wounded buffalo. A friend of Messiter's in Canada noted in a letter in 1872 that the hunter had found Milton's temper "most uncontrollable." Nothing of this antipathy reached the pages of Milton's book, of course, and Messiter too was generous in print, describing his antagonist as an old hand at buffalo running, "knowing as much about it as any man."

Indians at this time, like the Europeans, would hunt buffalo by charging them down on horseback with shotguns. But it had not always been this easy. Before guns and horses reached the North American plains they hunted them by running them over a cliff or into a gorge and finishing them off where they fell with knives and spears, or by running them through a funnel of fences into an enclosed pound and spearing them while they searched for a way out. Sometimes they chased the buffalo to these jumps and pounds and sometimes they lured them or frightened them there by dressing up in the mask and skin of a buffalo calf or a wolf: the ghost of a friend or the ghost of an enemy employed to the same effect.

It was always left to the women to cut up the animal wherever it had been killed and the old people and the weak and the widows were free to pick meat from the best carcasses on the field. No part of the buffalo was wasted. A fetus could be stitched to make a bag, a paunch to make a kettle, a horn enlisted to hold tobacco or carry a spark from a fire between camps, the skin dried and cured and stretched and used as a robe or as covering for a teepee, sinews extracted for bow-strings. The buffalo, as Milton learned, was the lifeblood of the Indian. Without it he was impotent on the plains, a ship without engine or sail. The downfall of the buffalo was the downfall of the Indian.

I climbed up across the north end of Jackson's Lake as close as I could tell to where Milton and Cheadle had gone, and it was hard going on the slope on the frozen earth with the top layer melting and slippery until at last the track levelled out on the plain. I didn't know whether I was on the old trail but I knew I was close. The Carlton Trail is so hard to pick up that close is about all I'd ever be. Everything was still and quiet apart from my footsteps and the alarm-call chatter of squirrels in the spruce and I felt like a trespasser in a world reserved for tranquility.

I flushed out a covey of prairie grouse from the hedge by the road. They wouldn't have stood a chance if Milton had been there with his double-barrelled Westley Richards. Between the gnarled trunks of old maples a snow hare made a grand effort through the snow. Growths of thin white-barked poplars lined the track like ghost armies. I came to a graveyard sectioned off from the surrounding farmland by spruce trees and an iron fence. It looked a lonely graveyard on the prairie with no attendant church and little traffic passing on the track. Many gravestones bore the same sur-names as others around them, Scottish, Irish and Eastern

European. Buried here were the pioneers who had followed the Carlton Trail a few years after Milton and settled beside it to make a life off the land they could not have had at home. They did not foresee the suffering, the harshness of winter, the crop disease and plagues of insects. Such hardships are written in this graveyard. People here speak of the resolution of the pioneers as others speak of the wartime heroics of their own grandparents. In Carberry, a small town to the west of the graveyard, a cairn that might have stood for the war dead reads: "This is dedicated to those early pioneers whose toil, courage and vision developed the big plain area."

I was standing outside the graveyard when a truck came up the dirt track, the first vehicle that day, and the driver stopped to inquire if I needed a lift. He was soft-spoken and kind-looking and it felt foolish to refuse a ride where rides were hard to come by. But I was happy in the quietness of the plain and I turned him down, wondering all the same if I'd regret it. I need not have worried. The next day, which was the spring equinox, I caught rides whenever I needed them, and my last one into Carberry was with a mother and her two small children. Either the stories of car-stealing hitchhikers had not reached this corner of Manitoba or my Union Jack had acquired impressive powers of persuasion.

You get a better feel for unbounded prairie skies when there are clouds about. Stacked-up clouds put a ceiling to the earth that beats down on you and holds you to the great flatness. It is the prairie uncertainty principle: beholden to the vertical, the horizontal falls from you forever. If you are not born to it it is hard to match such landscape unconfined to your perception of the world; a mouse brought up in a box is undone when presented with a wheel.

Milton's vision for these prairies – "65,000 square miles of a country of unsurpassed fertility, and abounding in mineral wealth, lies isolated from the world, neglected, almost unknown, although destined, at no distant period perhaps, to become one of the most valuable possessions of the British Crown" – was part of the fantasy that later drew the pioneers. For him, though, it was totally believable. How he loved the freedom of those untrammelled miles, how I love it too. It gets you in your stomach when you can see so far to the horizon you think you've got the curve of the Earth. There on the open plains you can belly out sweetness and obscenities and you won't even get back an echo. It is a great liberation. Did he thank for his deliverance the same God as I?

WILD WEST

Beyond Carberry, the Carlton Trail heads northwest across Manitoba's grid of roads through small towns, each with a single main street and a church for every denomination, towns where you can see the beginning and end in the same view and which begin and end in fields. It continues northwest for about fifty miles until it turns west again south of Shoal Lake – first settled six years after Milton's passing by Malcolm McMillan and his family, who would homestead there alone for seven years before the arrival of their first neighbour. Here, blistered and tramp-like, I booked into a motel for a night after two weeks sleeping out and looked forward to not being cold.

The next morning I was sitting in a café in Shoal Lake enjoying my first cooked breakfast since England when I was approached by a bustling middle-aged lady with excited eyes and a recent perm who sat down opposite me and started talking as if she had known me for years. "You have been noticed," she announced with a cheeriness more suited to the presentation of raffle prizes than an introduction over fried eggs. "You're not from around here." I looked at my outsized rucksack with its Union Jack and wondered at her insight. She turned around and nodded and winked at a table of ladies of similar appearance and cheeriness, all of whom nodded and winked in return as if party to some great conspiracy. "We," she declared triumphantly, "are the Coffee Mugs." Which explained everything. "And we are having a gathering." The Coffee Mugs, it transpired, are a group of women notorious in these parts for one thing: gossip. That morning, it seemed, I was their chosen subject. I suddenly wanted to run.

The lady opposite me must have been the chief Mug, for she was more bustling than the others, and she wore more badges. She cleared her throat and prepared to deliver judgment: "The Coffee Mugs have decided that you are far too young to be out by yourself at this time of year. We think you need some care and attention and we would like to take you home with us to ensure that you get it. Then we should like to telephone your mother to reassure her that you are safe." I shuddered. I would rather have been mothered by a herd of buffalo than by twenty clucking Canadian matriarchs. And I could imagine my mother's reaction to that telephone call: "Safe? Are you telling me he was unsafe? I'm flying over immediately."

I suppose I should have been insulted. Although I was thirty, I was always asked for ID in bars. The Coffee Mugs reckoned I was fifteen, and when I told them I was old enough to have watched Neil Armstrong on the moon they smiled disbelievingly and gave me a knowing nod. Then the senior Mug did the most annoying thing possible: she ruffled my hair. Even a fifteen-year-old would have been upset at this.

The senior Mug returned to her table and was shortly replaced by her second in command, who offered the same motherly sentiments as her leader, ruffling my hair as a sign-off. This ritual was repeated by the remaining Mugs until I felt like calling my mother myself. All that painful growing up undone at a single sitting, dominated forever by women. I had come to Canada for a masculine rite of passage and here I was being *femaled*. What would Milton have done? He would not have been comfortable: bush-hardened explorers, especially aristocratic ones, demanded more respect. I was eyeing the door when the Mugs rose as one and advanced on my table. "Hold out your hands!" cried the senior Mug. I obeyed, expecting to be smacked. Instead she poured into them a heap of coins. "We have taken a collection and would like to buy you your breakfast." I forgave them everything. To a lone traveller in a strange country such gestures mean a lot. Canadians are not short on friendliness. It must be harder to be lonely in the Canadian countryside than anywhere else on earth. That day I failed to pay for a single meal, thanks to the insistence and generosity of strangers.

The Coffee Mugs, I reasoned, had let me off lightly. They

didn't even ply me with sweets. One of them as she left promised not to call the police. She did, however, call the local newspaper, which arrived at the café as I was finishing my breakfast in the person of Darrell Nesbitt. Darrell is a reporter for the *Shoal Lake Star*, circulation two thousand. He also sells its advertising space. Conflicts of interest are not a problem on a small budget.

He said he was interested in what I was doing because it was a story close to the hearts of people in this community, many of whose ancestors had come from England and travelled here along the Carlton Trail. He wagered that for me to give up my job and follow my ancestor through Shoal Lake, on foot and in winter, it must be close to my heart too. He asked me about everything: my grandmother, Milton and what had driven him, what was driving me. He read the entry about Shoal Lake in Cheadle's diary, which pleased him greatly: "Very pretty, hills covered with trees around, beach sandy, water clear and good." It was predictably followed by: "A flock of geese came past us and I killed one, distance 68 yards, shot No. 3."

Darrell took me to see Ron Purdy, who is in his eighties and whose family has farmed around Shoal Lake since the early 1900s. The Carlton Trail crosses his land just south of the town and he says you can still see wheel ruts in places where it came up from the southeast and turned west through the "Narrows" at the south end of the lake on the way to Birdtail Creek and Birtle and Fort Ellice. Ron wanted to hear about England, for his family had suffered in the past for its loyalty to the Motherland. One of his distant uncles escaped from America down a river in a barrel during the War of Independence and was cut about the head when a federalist soldier stuck his bayonet through the top. All this in the name of King George.

Months later I would receive a copy of Darrell's article in the *Shoal Lake Star*. It takes up three-quarters of the front page and a third of page two, with photographs. I had expected a few paragraphs near the back. "One Man's Journey To Relive the Past" ran the headline. "Bond reached Shoal Lake on the morning of March 24 and was thrilled with the small town friendliness. . . . 'I find it most intriguing to sit and chat with local townsfolk as they seem to take pride in their history versus following maps and journal [sic],' Bond stated." Indeed. He mentioned everything, even my brother's impending wedding. It ended with a stomach-churning flourish: "If completed, Bond's journey will be a remarkable journey of faith and endurance. By tracing the path of his English ancestry, he will discover his past and its valuable connection to the current treasures of his heart and home." It must have delighted the Coffee Mugs.

I looked like toast gone too far on one side. I was always facing west and my left cheek was burnt by the sun mirrored off the snow to the south. After Shoal Lake I was on an approximation of the trail again, a quiet road between fields. The fields were cast in snow and set by the cold, moonscaped by the wind. The snow covered the lakes as well and the land in that abject uniformity and devoid of movement looked inappropriate for life of any kind.

And yet there was life, and it was not so lonely. The first geese had come in and were making a great to-do of finding open water, though they would lay their eggs before the ice broke so their young would be able to fly before it froze over again. They might have four months of open water. On this road I was courted by a bluebird, whose return to the prairies is considered a proclamation of spring, all metallic-blue sheen, fussing about between fenceposts as if appraising my credentials for being in such a place at such a time. I wasn't sure of my credentials. I hadn't seen anyone for miles. The only indicators of settlement were the grain elevators which are the tallest structures on the prairie artificial or natural and which you can see from twenty miles. It is comforting to see them because they suggest community, rail track, possibilities of shelter. People on the prairie get sentimental about grain elevators because they are high-standing testimony to the fruits of their hard labour. Grain buyers are making themselves unpopular by pulling down the old wooden elevators and erecting large concrete ones, each of which can serve several towns. Pull down an elevator and you pull something from the community, or so it feels. I walked to Birtle and I passed through and found a lift to St. Lazare near the Manitoba–Saskatchewan border, where the Carlton Trail crossed the Assiniboine River to the Hudson's Bay Company outpost at Fort Ellice – now destroyed.

The Fort Ellice logbook, held at the Hudson's Bay Company archives in Winnipeg, describes Milton and

Cheadle rather ignobly as "tourists on horseback," though they do appear to have treated the place as a hotel:

> Arrived at Fort; gates closed. Make a great hullabaloo. Doors open; drunken Indian, with only breechcloth on, immediately seizes my hand with friendly shake. The Factor Mr. Mackay appears without shoes or stockings. Provide us with dried meat & gallette & makes us beds on floor with blanket from store. . . . Did not appear at breakfast until 9. (Cheadle's journal)

Mr. Mackay was William, son of John, the first Fort Ellice factor. John Mackay had been popular with the Indians, who clearly were well disposed towards his son too. John was a skilled horseman and an expert with weapons and so could hardly have failed to win respect on the nineteenth-century plains. He was rumoured to have had Indian boys fire arrows at him that he fended off with his sword.

Such behaviour was not extravagant on the plains and neither was it unusual. If you were bad at looking after yourself you would not achieve much and you might not survive long. If you died on the plains west of Hudson's Bay it was not usually from old age. There were no cowboys for there were no cattle, but there were plenty of Indians and Europeans with guns and plenty of other ways to get into trouble: starvation, exposure, freezing, scurvy, riding accidents, drunkenness. Insane loneliness.

The forts of the Hudson's Bay Company were built as trading posts but in that wilderness they acted as refuges for all the players in the game. There you could rest up, see to your horses, receive mail, repair clothes, stock up for the few hundred miles to the next post. The only thing the forts were not always good for was protecting their inhabitants. Despite the customary palisade, they were hardly forts at all. One hundred years before Milton and Cheadle crossed Canada, a band of Chippewa Indians attacked Fort Michilimackinac on the Great Lakes during a game of *baggatiway* (lacrosse). It started when an Indian shot the ball over the palisade, which was a signal for the rest of the band to follow. They killed and scalped every Englishman they found inside.

The forts were better at providing food, or more precisely pemmican, which was stored in the cellars and also in the ground at strategic points along the Carlton Trail. It is still being retrieved by treasure-seekers and house-builders. Made as it was from pounded buffalo meat and boiled grease – some berries too if you were lucky – pemmican was hardly "high table," but if you were travelling it was your staple diet because it was highly nourishing and you didn't need much to keep you going. Milton and Cheadle rather took to it:

> It is uncommonly satisfying, and the most hungry mortal is able to devour but a very small portion. Many a time have we sat down half-famished, despising as insignificant the dish of pemmican set before us, and yet been obliged to leave the mess unfinished. It has, however, one drawback: it is very difficult of digestion, and a full meal of it is certain to cause considerable suffering to an unaccustomed stomach.

In *The Great Fur Opera*, a satire of the Hudson's Bay Company, author Kildare Dobbs offers a recipe for those wishing to make pemmican at home:

> Find some old, dried-out ends of meat and cut off the hard outside crusts. Pound these to dust in a mortar. Add mouldy raisins, buckshot, and a jug of melted, rancid animal fat. Sprinkle with long black hairs and poodle-clippings. Stir. Pour into an old shoe and refrigerate. After six months a greenish fur will have grown on the pemmican. Remove and keep this: it is pemmicillin. (*The Great Fur Opera*, Ronald Searle and Kildare Dobbs, 1970).

Sadly the Hudson's Bay Company no longer sells pemmican, and I couldn't persuade anybody to make me some.

Founded in 1670 by royal charter from Charles II, the Company behaved more like a government than a business – which, in fact, it was entitled to do, since its charter granted it control of all the land drained by rivers that flowed into Hudson's Bay. This area, known as Rupert's Land, was nearly a quarter of the North American continent. The Company could colonize, raise armies, build forts, pass laws – in short, govern. Its *raison d'être*, however, was trade. Europeans and Americans wanted beaverskin hats and fur coats. Indians wanted guns, blankets and knives. As markets go, it was deliciously untapped. Just about anything an Indian could trap, snare or shoot would fetch a price at a Hudson's Bay Company trading post: black bear, brown bear, polar bear, badger, buffalo, beaver, caribou, red deer, moose, elk, fisher, black fox, silver fox, red fox, white fox, blue fox, lynx, marten, muskrat, otter, seal, whale, wolf, wolverine. Ivory from the walrus. The feathers of large birds. In exchange, Indians would choose from the company's stores or the travel-chests of its traders weapons, beads, hats, blankets, tobacco, thread, cloth, tools, gunpowder, shirts, shoes, lace. Kettles and pots. The furnishings of a civilization to which they would forevermore be beholden. Today the Hudson's Bay Company runs a chain of department stores. In some respects it always has done.

In the beginning the company recruited all its fur traders from the Orkney Islands, whose inhabitants could apparently endure any hardship or antagonism and still remain peaceful. It was not a civilized job:

> Early Company servants sometimes froze to death. Survivors had learned the secret of keeping warm: BE DIRTY. Nothing is more calorific than a thick coating of filth. The trader's hands and face were black as a chimney-sweep's, his clothes greasy as a butcher's. . . . The traders' hairy appearance could lead to misunderstanding. In September, 1800, three grizzly bears tried to climb into a York boat with the Company's Peter Fidler and crew. "These," he primly reported, "was the most daring Bears any of us had ever seen." (*The Great Fur Opera*)

While Milton was polite about the way the Hudson's Bay Company was run and the way it treated the Indians, he railed against its monopoly on trade. He noted that it actively discouraged immigration, endeavouring to keep the country as a preserve for fur-bearing animals and opposing development of any kind. What a waste, he thought:

> From Red River to the Rocky Mountains, along the banks of the Assiniboine and the fertile belt of the Saskatchewan, at least sixty millions of acres of the richest soil lie ready for the farmer when he shall be allowed to enter in and possess it. This glorious country, capable of sustaining an enormous population, lies utterly useless, except for the support of a few Indians, and the enrichment of the shareholders of the Last Great Monopoly.

Milton the free-trader. Was it trade that bothered him, or the thought that a few unelected directors in an office in London could dictate the future of an entire country and deny everyone else the opportunity to benefit? He dedicates several pages to his rant against the Company. It is all very objectively argued, but I suspected the root of it was rather more personal. He had come to Canada seeking some kind of liberation. He was escaping, among other things, a monopoly on his behaviour imposed by his oligarchy of a family, and by English society in general. How irritating it must have been to find Canada, supposedly land of the free, in the grip of another English fist.

With people like Milton about the monopoly could not last, and in truth the first nail was already in the coffin. In 1811, Lord Selkirk had bought from the Company 116,000 square miles of land on the Red River south of Lake

Winnipeg on which he hoped to settle hundreds of poor Scottish peasants who had been cleared from their homes by his fellow noblemen. The rival North West Company, formed by the leading fur traders of Montreal in 1784 and described by its enemies as "a syndicate of lawless and ruthless racketeers" – it was incorporated into the Hudson's Bay Company in 1821 – feared that Selkirk's colony would disrupt their trade and twice tried to destroy it. The Earl, resolute, hired a legion of Swiss soldiers from the De Meuron regiment in Montreal, seized the North West Company's headquarters at Fort William and re-established his Red River settlement.

The settlement and Fort Garry – built there in 1822 – from then on fed the colonization of the prairies and the land to the west of the Rocky Mountains. After Confederation in 1867, when the eastern provinces of Nova Scotia, New Brunswick and Upper and Lower Canada (Ontario and Quebec) were united under a single Dominion government in Ottawa, the Hudson's Bay Company's monopoly began to look a little ridiculous. Even the Company acknowledged this, and in 1869 it "sold" Rupert's Land for £300,000 to the British government, which transferred it – and the bill – to Canada. Overnight, the Dominion had increased the size of its territory nearly tenfold, and the British government, paranoid for some time that America would annex the West, could relax a little. There were dissenters, of course, and Louis Riel's independent-minded Métis rebels gave Ottawa a hard time until they were defeated at Batoche in 1885.

The Wild West by that time was well on the way to being tamed. It would have been no challenge to two roughshod sons of the Empire cutting passage. The early 1860s was a better time for Milton and Cheadle to be there. They could lend themselves to its opening.

Rested and fillered up with pemmican, they rode out from Fort Ellice on the Carlton Trail heading northwest and into the end of summer. They rode through prairie parkland broken up with lakes and they flushed wildfowl from the wayside like moths out of heather: Canada geese, snow geese, mallards, canvasbacks, various kinds of pochards, blue-winged teal, common teal. Milk and honey of the plains. An abundance that conservationists would wonder at today. Not that Milton was pondering conservation of any kind:

> The ducks at this season are most delicious, possessing much of the ordinary flavour of the wild bird, with all the fatness and delicacy of the tame one. The broods of prairie grouse were already full grown, and very plentiful. When driven into the little round copses of aspen which are such a prominent feature of the park country, they afforded capital sport.

As far as I could tell Milton and Cheadle had shot their way right across the prairie and they were still shooting when they reached Fort Carlton on the North Saskatchewan on September 26, 1862, thirty-four days, five hundred miles and a great number of dead ducks, prairie hens and buffalo from the Red River Settlement.

Manitobans say their plains are best crossed in a hurry. There is little that is comforting about them in winter and it is a battle getting across them even on flat unbroken roads. Scarcity of people, uninhibited winds. The birds and animals, rationed on water and prey, have a hard time of it as well. Flocks of snow buntings roll against the wind like the breaking crests of waves. Abandoned wooden barns are twisted into holocaust grimaces.

There are cairns marking where the Carlton Trail crosses the road in parts of Saskatchewan but the closest I could get to following it directly was to walk the Canadian National Railway. This is not recommended in travel books. To do it you have to step on the sleepers between the rails, for much of the land is marshy and the sleepers are out of the snow and solid. When I first started doing this beyond Esterhazy in Saskatchewan I heard ghosts of trains every minute and had to turn to check I wasn't about to be run down. But the real trains are mostly slow freights and a hundred or more container-cars long and you can hear them for miles. Between the trains on the line there is a great stillness.

With the ice creasing up and thawing on the fields you can feel the land letting go a little. You can hear it in the snow if you lie down and hold your breath as the crystals melt and the lattice that holds it all together collapses. The crows had been in for a while, but they say it snows four times after the crows arrive before spring starts properly, and it had snowed only twice. The geese were coming in from the south and they were not shy in celebrating. For several days I woke, walked and bedded down to geese music, sleeping in copses of poplar and red willow and wild rose with the hips frozen on the branches. Every morning when I woke and for all of those days the only clouds were those nailed to the horizon. It felt as if the whole land was serenading spring. I was marshalled by deer up the line and they would stay well ahead of me and sometimes ballet across the line in high freeze-frame leaps. They would do this in front of trains and not always make it, for I'd come on a deer carcass attended by crows with some distance between its front- and hindquarters.

I managed three miles an hour for seven hours a day on the line and that was enough. I envied Milton for having it easy over this part, in summer and with horses. It would have looked different to him. In those days the Carlton Trail ran through knee-deep prairie grass. The Canadian National Railway runs across Saskatchewan through farmland. If Milton had done it today he wouldn't have been allowed to hunt, but he couldn't have complained too much about that since he had envisaged agriculture as the best thing for this land.

In early April I reached Melville, population under five thousand yet masquerading as a city. At the beginning of the platform I was met by the stationmaster and part-time conductor (called himself a semi-conductor), who had been watching me come up the tracks. "That, sir, is a most unusual way of arriving at a railway station," he said. In the bank the lady behind the till asked me why I looked as if I had walked from Manitoba. When I told her, she looked horrified and gave me a bag of miniature Easter eggs. It was the Sunday before Easter. I thanked her and mumbled that they would do for food for that day at least, and she looked horrified again. Then she began to look sympathetic. I remembered the Coffee Mugs and, fearing I was about to have my hair ruffled, took the money and ran.

Through the Touchwood Hills northwest of Melville I treated myself and rode on a train and revelled in having to do nothing for my miles except pay for them. The line and the Carlton Trail part company after this and so I got off and hitchhiked up towards Fort Carlton, losing the trail for a considerable distance among the roads and fields and picking it up again before the southern branch of the Saskatchewan River. Approaching the replica Hudson's Bay Company fort that now stands at Carlton – the one that Milton visited was burnt down – I was in the cart ruts of the old trail, hard-sculpted under the dead grass.

The site, beside the North Saskatchewan River, was deserted, for it was off-season. I camped beneath the fort, which looked faithful enough with its stockade and lookout towers, and woke in the night to the manic whoops and cackles of coyotes and the foghorn hoot of an owl. The ice was splintering on the Saskatchewan and breaking up in great blocks paraded away downstream in the Arctic version of a lavaform cascade, the snow reflecting moonshine as if fired by its own energy source and the moon so bright it might have started another day on the back of the old one. It was a desolate scene compared with Milton's first night at Carlton on the other side of winter in 1862:

> A ball was got up by the half-breeds in honour of our visit. Mr Lillie [the factor] gave up his best room for the purpose, and we provided the refreshment, in the shape of rum; the expectation that we should do so being no doubt one of the greatest attractions the entertainment offered. The men appeared in gaudy array, with beaded firebag, gay sash, blue or scarlet leggings, girt below the knee with beaded garters, and moccasins elaborately embroidered; the women in short, bright-coloured skirts, showing the richly-embroidered leggings, and white moccasins of cariboo-skin, beautifully worked with flowery patterns in beads, silk, and moose hair. Some of the young girls were good-looking, but many of them were disfigured by goitre.

Cheadle missed all of this, being "not in the humour for gaiety." It is hard to imagine less-likely travelling companions. Had Milton ever been "not in the humour for gaiety" when presented with music and women?

INDIAN WINTER

Milton and Cheadle had planned to cross the Rocky Mountains through the Yellowhead Pass, "with the design of discovering the most direct route through British territory to the gold regions of Cariboo." This was all terribly worthy, but there was a problem. It was nearly winter, and they couldn't cross the mountains in winter.

So they brewed up another wildcat scheme to pass the time while they waited to carry out the wildcat scheme for which they had come. Considering Fort Carlton too unadventurous, they rode north across the Saskatchewan River and then for four days to the Shell River – west of present-day Prince Albert – and on to a lake with promontories and a meadow they named La Belle Prairie on account of, well, its beauty. They crossed this meadow and, "as we crossed it, we remarked to one another what a magnificent site for a house one of the promontories would be." So they built a house on one of the promontories – a rude cabin fifteen feet by thirteen and six feet high and engineered with considerable skill by Milton from poplar logs, mud and marsh grass and complete with chimney. La Ronde named it Fort Milton. Here they lived for the next six months through the coldest winter either of them had known. If they were counting on hardship as cardinal to their mission then October to spring at La Belle Prairie should suit.

It was often below minus 30°C and they both suffered frostbite and Milton erysipelas, in which his eye reddened and swelled in abomination at the cold. Cheadle's beard and moustache frosted up with ice-balls the size of a fist. The preserving oil froze in their pipes. If they touched a finger to a piece of iron the two would bond.

> Clothed in three or four flannel shirts, one of duffel, and a leather shirt; our hands encased in "mittaines," or large gloves of moose-skin lined with duffel, made without fingers, large enough to admit of being easily doffed on occasion, and carried slung by a band round the neck; our feet swathed in bands of duffel, covered by enormous moccasins; and our ears and necks protected by a curtain of fur, we were yet hardly able to keep warm with the most active exercise. . . . With a roaring fire, sleeping fully clothed, with the addition of two buffalo robes and two blankets, it was impossible to keep warm.

They heard stories of a train of dogs on the trail to Fort Garry frozen to death upright in their harnesses and still attached to the sleigh. The dogs had died lying down but some traveller with a macabre sense of humour had stood them up. A sculptural apocalypse. Jacques Cartier, the French navigator who in 1535 "discovered" Canada for the King of France, maintained that words could be frozen on the lips of a man at the end of a Canadian autumn and hang in the air until the spring, when they could be heard by other men. A fantastic cold breeds a fantastic mythology.

They would have had a far harder time of it without La Ronde, whose expertise in hunting buffalo and in trapping helped to keep them in meat. At Fort Carlton they had hired another Métis called Athanase Bruneau, though he did not quite fit the role of "housemaid and laundress" that Milton had in mind for him. So he hired a local hand:

Milton took the opportunity afforded by the visit of an Indian and his squaw, to engage the latter for a general washing and house-cleaning. Although it was night when they arrived, the woman set to work immediately, diligently melting snow at a roaring fire for hours, and when about midnight she had obtained a sufficient supply of water, proceeded to scrub blankets and clothes. Milton expostulated, and suggested she should retire to rest, but in vain. The splashing and scrubbing went on without cessation, and sleep was impossible. At length Milton, driven to desperation, jumped out of bed, threw away all the water, and put out the fire. The squaw thereupon retired to rest in much astonishment, and for a time all was still. Presently, however, when she imagined Milton had fallen asleep, she quietly got up, and re-commenced her labours. The unhappy retainer of her services was fairly beaten, and compelled to resign himself to his fate, venting many maledictions on the untimely industry of his servant.

Thus did Milton demonstrate the capacity of the English aristocracy for creating abroad an approximation of the way things were at home. One hundred miles from the nearest house and several hundred from anything he would recognize as civilization he had managed to secure the services of a maid.

The fact that Milton did not think twice about employing a Cree Indian woman to do his washing up was typical of Victorian attitudes towards Natives, but unlike many of his countrymen he did not treat all Indians as his servants. He may have referred to their neighbours at La Belle Prairie as "*les sauvages*" and "*les sauvagesses*," but he was also in awe of them. He dressed in their moccasins and deerhide shirts. He made extensive notes on obscure aspects of their lives and gave public lectures on these when he got back to England. He was impressed with their hair, which he considered "most luxuriant indeed it is not very infrequent to meet with both men and women whose hair when platted [sic], which is the usual mode of coiffeur amongst them, reaches the ground." Baldness and grey hair were virtually unknown among them, except in cases of extreme starvation.

The only exception he came across was a woman held to be 148 years old, whose hair was nearly white. He admired the Cree for their lavish hospitality, "sometimes even getting considerably into debt to do honour to their guests whoever they may be"; for their honesty, "in which they equal if not excel almost all the other inhabitants of British North America"; and for their engineering skills, in particular for an all-purpose knife with a handle angled out for a more powerful grip which Milton declared could do "as much as a whole tool chest for a white man." (His praise of the Indian, it should be noted, did not extend to the French "half-breeds" – though he must have considered La Ronde a special case – whom he described as "taking no pride in fishing and farming. This arrives from their unparraleled [sic] love of idleness and the extreme depth of their igno-rance – which two things I have never seen or heard of being equalled in any people.")

Despite his imperialistic leanings – and despite the editor of the French edition of *The North-West Passage by Land* describing the journey as "*une nouvelle preuve de la superi-orité morale que la race blanche a sur les autres*" – Milton was no "civilizer" of Indians, and he was no missionary. At La Belle Prairie he learnt to speak Cree fluently and ended up spending as much time with the Natives as he did with Cheadle. He saw them as victims of the prejudices of the age, outcasts in their homeland like him. Kindred spirits drawn together in the winter wilderness. He focused his energies in particular on a mysterious Cree woman called Dalilah. She appears nowhere in *The North-West Passage by*

Land and in none of Milton's letters, but she crops up occasionally in Cheadle's journal and the intimation is always that she is Milton's lover, mainly because of Cheadle's inevitable disapproval: "Find Dalilah [in cabin]; disgusted." "Expostulate with Milton about D." "In a fix about D." He could bring himself to spell out her name only once, thereafter using her initial or referring to her as "*la petite sauvagesse.*" Was a mixed-race union too much for Cheadle to bear or was he simply bewildered at his young charge running amok? The episode is hardly surprising since it seems inconceivable that Milton could spend six months in a snowbound cabin with women within striking distance and not lay his hands on one of them. He was a Fitzwilliam after all, if an unusual one. News of the liaison must have carried home, for when he died his family wrote to James Dreaver, an Indian trader who was married to the daughter of a local Cree chief called Mistawasis, asking whether he knew if Milton had any descendants in Canada who might be entitled to a legacy. Dreaver reported that, while Milton did indeed have an Indian wife, he had sadly left no heirs.

How disappointing. Of all the twists in Milton's tale the one that would sell it and have Hollywood chasing film rights was an affair in the backwoods and a Fitzwilliam–Cree lineage. Where would that have put the Earldom? Some hundred miles north of Saskatoon, no doubt. Imagine my grandmother's excitement at that. At least the affair had happened, wintered-in and cabin-bound, or tepee-bound, although minus 30°C might have taken the sting out of it. Imagine my grandmother's excitement at *that*. I was surprised she had never heard about it, or even made up a version. It was just her kind of story.

Milton and Cheadle befriended several Cree but they befriended one family above all. The old man Kekekooarsis, or "Child of the Hawk" on account of his beak-like nose, his son-in-law Keenamontiayoo (the "Long Neck"), and Keenamontiayoo's fourteen-year-old son Misquapamayoo ("The Thing One Catches a Glimpse Of") lived by White Fish Lake nearby and became even more crucial than La Ronde and Bruneau to the Englishmen's survival, though their first meeting was inauspicious:

> In a weak moment we promised to make him [Keke-kooarsis] a present of a small quantity of rum. Alas! mistaken generosity, fruitful of anxiety and trouble! The old gentleman became all excitement, said we were the best fellows he had met for many a day, adding that if he might venture to offer a suggestion, it would be that we should fetch the fire-water immediately. . . . [Soon] they were already half drunk, singing away the Indian song without words, and clamorous for more rum. . . . We doled out another small quantity, as the only way to get rid of them. How they chuckled and hugged the pot! exclaiming, "Tarpwoy! tarpwoy!" (It is true! it is true!) hardly able to believe the delightful fact. . . . Boys rode off as couriers in all directions to carry the welcome tidings to their friends in the neighbourhood. Before long men came galloping up from different quarters, and these were presently followed by squaws and children, all eager to taste the pleasure-

giving fire-water, and our lodge was soon crowded with importunate guests.

But things calmed down, Milton and Cheadle buried their rum and the Indians set about teaching them how to hunt and trap. Cheadle became known as Muskeeky Okey Mow, or "My Master, the Great Medicine," and Milton as Soniow Okey Mow, or "Great Golden Chief," which would have pleased him enormously. Keenamontiayoo would take them off for days into the woods with pemmican and tea slung in a blanket across their backs and a gun and some traps, snowshoeing out into the silence and stillness, an Indian file of wild men bent on meat and fur. They set "deadfall" traps from saplings and logs that would crush a marten or fisher and spring-loaded steel traps for beavers, foxes and wolves. They would eat the animals they caught but Milton's first concern was their fur, especially that of the silver fox and the cross fox and the fisher and marten and mink, which he felt sure would be "gratefully received when presented to dear friends of the fair sex at home." With Keenamontiayoo Milton was in good hands, for the man had a reputation as a hunter among many Indian hunters of that region. Even La Ronde was impressed, especially with the Indian's ability to walk for days a straight course in a single direction in dense forest under cloud with no wind and no distinguishing features for reference, neither hill nor lake, an ability La Ronde considered innate and that no man could learn.

The Indians in this place were Woods Cree. They were different to the Cree of the plains, who were horsemen and buffalo-runners and hostile. The Woods Cree were solitary trappers and hunters and lived off moose and the occasional buffalo, and they were inveterate traders. There was little about the habits and preferences of fur-bearing animals that they did not understand and no animal that they did not know how to dupe into taking bait – apart from one. The wolverine – or carcajou, or North American glutton, or skunk bear as it has variously been called – was his nemesis, pillaging his traps for bait and prey and rarely caught. The Indians called the animal *Kekwaharkess*, "The Evil One." Other animals would flee the scent of man. The wolverine sought it. Once a wolverine had found a trap-run – and they frequently found Milton's and Cheadle's – the best thing was to find somewhere else to set the traps, for if you baited them up on the original run the wolverine would demolish them every time. Furthermore, it would never touch poisoned bait. Milton and Cheadle, despite going hungry because of it, were impressed:

> Strange stories are related by the trappers of the extraordinary cunning of this animal, which they believe to possess a wisdom almost human. . . . In one instance La Ronde, when every device to deceive his persecutor had been at once seen through, and utterly futile, he adopted the plan of placing a gun in a tree, with the muzzle pointing vertically downwards upon the bait [a string connecting bait to trigger]. The gun was suspended from a branch, at such a height that the animal could not reach it without jumping. . . . Now, the wolverine is an animal troubled with exceeding curiosity.

Anything suspended almost out of reach generally offers an irresistible temptation. But in this case the carcajou restrained his curiosity and hunger for the time, climbed the tree, cut the cords which bound the gun, which thus tumbled harmless to the ground, and then, descending, secured the bait without danger.

If certain animals were a Cree Indian's enemy, others were his friends. From them he could learn the nature of country close at hand or of what was coming. The flight of the crane at the end of the summer would tell him how long he had before winter. The cry of the loon would tell him of prey near at hand, or of coming winds.

The success or failure of an Indian in hunting would determine whether or not his family would starve, and it was inconceivable that this responsibility should come down solely to luck and his own skill. Superstition and spirituality would bear the brunt of it. If the Great Spirit, or *Manitou*, was pleased, then he would provide. Once when Keenamontiayoo failed to find a moose after two days of trying he returned to White Fish Lake to perform an invocation:

Drums were brought out, and rattles made of bladders with pebbles in them, "medicine" belts of wolf skin donned, and other "medicine" or magic articles, such as ermine skins, and muskrat skins covered with beads. The Hunter and his father-in-law drummed and rattled, and sang songs, finishing, after some hours, by a long speech which they repeated together, in which they promised to give some of the best meat to the Manitou if he granted success, and to compose a new song in his praise.

By the following evening he had two moose.

For all this the Cree must have had a hard time in pursuit of game, for Cheadle in his diary writes of many starving. In February when he and Keenamontiayoo killed a few stray buffalo, the only ones for hundreds of miles, several families of gaunt, emaciated Indians – "a spectral cavalcade" – came into their camp to share the meat, "almost literally skin and bone, with hide drawn tightly and unpadded over ribs and spine." Several winters previously Keenamontiayoo had lost consciousness through lack of food and would have died had not a party of Hudson's Bay Company men been passing.

This winter they were starving at the forts too. At Fort Egg Lake they had to boil down a buffalo hide. Hunters sent out by Fort Carlton were forced to eat their dogs. Milton and Cheadle, through good luck and good British planning as they would have it, went hungry but never starved, though they had to keep at the hunting and once made a dash to Fort Carlton for emergency supplies of pemmican. They even sent La Ronde on a two-month dogsleigh round trip to Fort Garry for flour and tea. They might want for meat and fat and scrape to stay alive but, by Jove, they'd miss tea over their dead bodies (and, so it would seem, La Ronde's).

✥

You might think they would be at each other's throats holed up in Fort Milton through such a winter, Cheadle raging at Milton's reluctance to get up in the mornings and his indiscretions with his Indian girl, Milton at Cheadle's puritanism and his schoolmastering (he was, after all, his doctor), but you won't find any mention of a quarrel in *The North-West Passage by Land*. There is more honesty in Cheadle's diary, in which he writes several times of "warm" discussions with his friend – interpret those as hot. Apart from Dalilah, the thing about Milton that consistently discomfited Cheadle (and would do so for the rest of the journey) was his grumbling when physically challenged:

Friday, January 2nd – Milton soon after the start very unhappy & having serious misgivings that the two Indians who were leading would not think it necessary to stop for dinner, wearying me with his complaints & curses that he had ever come & wanting to stop and make a fire with every rotten stick he saw.

Tuesday, January 13th – Milton wearing me with fruitless questions every few minutes whether we are nearly there; wondering whether Keenamontiayoo has lost his way. Groaning & moaning as he walks up every hill, & I almost quarrel with him, using very strong language occasionally. He declares he is killing himself, & shall be laid up for a week &c, &c. I pooh-pooh it.

It is true that Milton liked to eat on time. It is true that he would sooner have ridden a horse to the end of the street than walked the distance. He also liked to get his own way. He must have been tricky. Cheadle, though, had a talent for pooh-poohing. He pooh-poohed anything off-line or liberal. He pooh-poohed most patronizingly Milton's suggestion that he might come back to La Belle Prairie to live some day: "Milton very full of plans, drawing ground-plan of prospective house, giving prospective wages & provisions to prospective men. I moralise on the uncertainty of all things & strain hard to catch philosophy." (Cheadle's diary)

The point, of course, was that there was no philosophy, but there was great heart. Milton was full of excitement in the love of the wilderness and he would make his plans in that spirit and damn the "sensible" course. I don't think Cheadle realized how deep it went. Milton would never return to La Belle Prairie, but he would return to the Canadian wilderness to live when he was thirty-two and his son and heir was born there. Though Cheadle took the journey seriously, to him it was a job to do, time out from the real thing. To Milton it was the real thing, or the makings of it.

They appear unsuited to each other but in many ways it would be difficult to find a better match. In Milton there was all heart and passion, in Cheadle all head; in the one creation, in the other control. They were Dionysus and Apollo of Greek mythology, the contrarian sons of Zeus who reigned together. Dionysus is chaos, intoxication, inspiration, ecstasy, energy; Apollo is order, symmetry, balance, moderation. These opposites are found in all mythologies, and they are always partners. You find them implicit in the physical world too, and in the human condition. The flux of quantum physics takes place against an ordered universe; some of the greatest poems follow a rigid structure of rhythm and rhyme. Milton and Cheadle's partnership may not have been a work of art, but it worked pretty well. In *The North-West Passage by Land* they acknowledge the balance of roles at Fort Milton: "Milton presided over the culinary department, in which he displayed great skill and ingenuity, severely taxed to make a variety of dishes out of such limited resources, while Cheadle was hewer of wood and drawer of water."

While you might not expect bashfulness from Milton where there was talent to flaunt, he seems worthy of this boast. He conjured up delicacies that bestowed on the wilderness the mark of an English home: pembina jam, galettes, pancakes and – his most celebrated creation – a plum pudding: "From a modest distrust of his own skill, Milton had hitherto hesitated to attempt so high a flight; but encouraged by a series of successes in the savoury branch of the culinary art, and urged by the eager solicitations of Cheadle, he at length consented to attempt a plum pudding." Since a modest distrust of his own skill was an unlikely affliction for Milton, I suspected the delay was down to a lack of proper ingredients. Nevertheless, two months after Christmas he drummed up currants, raisins, flour, sugar and bits of shrivelled fruit and set to work:

It proved delicious beyond all anticipation, in spite of certain drawbacks in the shape of caps, buck-shot, and fragments of tobacco, which we discovered in it. We had fondly hoped to finish it at a sitting, but it was a very Brobdingnagian pudding, and we were reluctantly compelled to leave a portion unconsumed. We passed the night somewhat restlessly, partly caused perhaps by the indigestible character of our evening meal, but principally from impatience for the morning to arrive, that we might repeat the delights of the previous evening. When day began to break, each watched the movements of the other with anxious distrust, and before it was fairly light both jumped out of bed at the same moment, each fearful he might lose his share of the delicious breakfast. Never did schoolboy view with such sincere regret the disappearance of his last morsel of cake, as we did when sighing over the last mouthful of that unequalled pudding.

Reassuringly, the operation had also cleared up any lingering feelings of modesty.

Thus despite their differences – or because of them – they survived each other. It seems Milton was quite affectionate towards Cheadle, who was to a great extent his protector. Cheadle in his diary notes Milton's enthusiastic reaction to his return from a hunting trip: "Hello Cheadle devlish glad to see you back, all alone here for 4 days & getting very 'down in the mouth.'" Earlier Milton had engineered a special fur attachment to Cheadle's cap to stop his ears getting cold; on the prairies he had carved him a rough smoking-pipe, which for some time was kept at the Museum of Civilization in Ottawa in the mistaken belief that it had been carved by an Indian.

And when equanimity eluded them there were plenty of ways to let out aggression, such as driving a dogsleigh through the woods:

> Of all things in the world calculated to ruffle the most even temper, driving a worthless train of Indian dogs stands unequalled. It may be doubted whether the most rigidly pious evangelical would be able to keep his lips free from language unbecoming his profession, under circumstances trying almost beyond human endurance; and indeed it is said that one of the missionaries on the Saskatchewan, a most worthy and pious man, when travelling with some of his flock in the winter, astonished and horrified his companions by suddenly giving vent, in his distraction, to most dreadful anathemas against his dogs.

Milton got his own special chance to huff and puff with the arrival one evening of their colleague Charles Messiter, buffalo-hunter, Indian-baiter and goader of English lords. Messiter was wintering southwest of Fort Milton in the Thickwood Hills so that he could hunt with the renowned Indian hunter Ahtahkakoohp, or "Star Blanket." He had come up to La Belle Prairie to trade with the Woods Cree and was thus set to antagonize Milton:

Monday, December 29th – Milton & Messiter rush off straightway to Keenamontiayoo's, the former in an awful excitement about Messiter getting the furs there, & threatening strychnine & all kinds of devilry. I laugh at him, tell him that is all nonsense & rubbish & advise him not to make a fool of himself.

Tuesday, December 30th – Milton comes in before dark in great excitement. They had come to knives drawn about the martens the night before, both having skins owed. . . . Milton vowing to poison again. . . . I write up journal & listen to Milton's anathemas against Messiter; very tired of it. (Cheadle's diary)

Messiter thought little of Fort Milton, describing it in his *Sport and Adventures among the North-American Indians* as "a much less pretending house" than his. This Milton would have taken as a considerable insult.

Messiter had lost none of his talent for falling out with Indians. A few weeks earlier he had almost died in his hut one night after hitting Ahtahkakoohp in the face in response to some insult. This was hot-headed to say the least, for at the time Ahtahkakoohp was accompanied by six other half-drunk Indians, who at Messiter's punch drew their knives and started laying into him. They would have run him through had it not been for the intervention of a giant Métis named Tamboot, who was known to have killed a man with a single punch. Messiter had been kind to Tamboot and the colossus chose to show his appreciation then by picking up Ahtahkakoohp and smashing him against the wall of the hut, marking out for similar treatment anyone who dared lay a hand on his friend. Later that year Messiter would again cheat death at the hand of an Indian, shooting dead a Sioux chief who had swung at him with a club and having to ride for four days to escape his enraged band. ("A good many shots were fired at me during the first few hundred yards, but I lay forward on my horse, and they all missed me, though some of them seemed to come pretty close.")

Evening entertainment at Fort Milton was more restrained, centring as it did on the antics of Rover the dog:

> His performances were an unfailing source of wonder and delight to our Indian visitors, who never tired of watching him stand on his head, walk about on his hind legs, or sit up in the begging attitude. But one of his feats elicited loud "wah! wahs!" and "aiwarkakens!" their expressions of astonishment. This was watching a piece of meat placed on the floor, or sitting with it balanced on his nose. They could not understand how a dog could be taught to refrain from seizing it at once, instead of waiting for the word of command.

How Natives and Englishmen did astonish each other.

THE SWEET-GRASS TRAIL

The story of what happened to Keenamontiayoo's band of Indians in the decades after Milton left and what is still happening is hard to believe if heard in entirety, such is the magnitude of the changes wrought on them. It can be understood as a series of upheavals levied by nation upon nation and predictable one to the other, but the outcome seems too preposterous to be real and Milton could never have foretold it. Where there was freedom there are fences; where there were teepees there are bungalows; where there was the Manitou there is God the Father; where there were buffalo there are none. Where there was starvation there is none.

La Belle Prairie was never called that by anyone before Milton or after and it took some finding. Four days' ride north of Carlton and over the Shell River there are *belles prairies* by the dozen and most of them are beside lakes. This is the top edge of the plains and the bottom of the northern boreal forest and the landscape is in confusion – aspen mixed with spruce, moose and black bear with white-tailed deer, marsh and lake and river with pasture and arable land. And how has the land changed since 1863, what lakes have retreated and what advanced, what rivers changed course; what land is cultivated that then was forested?

In the middle of May I travelled to the town of Shell Lake on the Shell River, which is on the old cart trail from Fort Carlton. I stayed in a small room above the only bar in town and after two weeks I knew all the drinkers and had met many others. I told them Milton's story. While they were all as helpful as they could be and interested in why an Englishman should have wanted to sit out a winter in these parts and why another should wish to follow him a hundred and thirty-odd years later, none of them had the faintest clue as to what I was talking about.

Whenever I showed my copy of *The North-West Passage by Land* to white Canadians they would remark on its binding and look at the photographs, perhaps read a few sentences. Whenever I showed it to Cree Indians they would study it intently, read entire passages before commenting and pass it between themselves like some ancestral text. The first time this happened was in the bar with Debbie Watson and her uncle Vern Johnstone and his wife Ruth and some others, all of whom live on the Mistawasis Indian Reserve south of Shell River. The book was out of my hands before it dawned on me that Milton's descriptions of the Cree might not be appreciated by modern Indians, especially Kekekooarsis's antics with the fire-water and all the references to "les petites sauvagesses." If they were offended they never showed it; probably they had seen much worse. Indeed they were enthralled by Milton's stories for they were of Cree before settlement, a time even their grandparents had not known. Vern picked out Tamboot, the giant who had finished a man with a single punch, and there followed several claims around the table for descent from this Indian.

It can be hard to trace a Native line, for little is written down and it used not to be done to speak the names of the dead. In addition, by "grandfather" a Cree does not always mean his parent's father, nor by "grandmother" his parent's mother. Vern decided to take me to his sister, Leonie, for while he recognized none of the names and none of the places in Milton's book he reckoned that she would know if anyone did.

Leonie is in her sixties and she has eleven children, forty-eight grandchildren and several great-grandchildren. She is a former band chief and a cheerful and inveterate talker but above all she is the daughter of the late Norman Johnstone, one of the most respected Cree chiefs and storytellers of his time. Norman's grandfather was a Scottish doctor called Edward Johnstone, who married chief Mistawasis's granddaughter after seeing her in a fur-trading store near Shell River. In such ways in that era did many Cree lineages merge with European. Leonie said Norman always reckoned that Mistawasis himself had European blood, for he had blue eyes.

Leonie has a photograph of her father when he was a boy, standing in the snow outside a log cabin near Prince Albert where they used to live, and she explained that they had kept a monkey inside the cabin and they had taught this monkey how to put logs on the fire to keep it burning while they were out hunting. One day in the winter after several days out they came back and found the monkey frozen to death in front of the unlit fire and the fireplace crammed with logs. They had taught it how to feed a fire but they had not taught it how to light one. Debbie said Norman used to tell her such stories several times over so that she could learn them by heart. This is the oral tradition. Write them down and you lose half the picture.

Norman died on Leonie's birthday. I told her I knew how it felt since my father had died on mine. We agreed that it ended up giving the day rather a fine significance. Death into life and all that. I sat at Leonie's table with several of her children and a good many of her grandchildren causing chaos at our feet. All the adults were smoking. As far as I could tell they were all women. There were things happening wherever you looked and it was a happy circus. Ivan, Leonie's husband, emerged from the kitchen wearing an apron and declaring, if he might get a word in, that the white man would never have settled the Indians had he understood the domestic anarchy it would cause. "Before, a man had five or six wives and they all did all the cooking. Now a man has one wife and *he* has to do all the cooking. Some wives today even seem to have five or six husbands." Leonie shooed him back to the kitchen. She turned to me and said that, while it was a pity she did not know the people or the places in my book, it was no matter for in a Cree household it was a tradition that a male visitor married a girl of the house. So why didn't I make my choice from this here assembly and pick up where my ancestor left off? There followed much cackling from the assembly. I told Leonie that it was a very tempting offer but that before I made the decision I first needed to find out where exactly my ancestor had left off. Then I needed to check with my girlfriend in England. Leonie seemed satisfied, and shooed me into the kitchen to help her husband.

I spent the first two weeks in the area being passed from family to family and getting nowhere. I began to wonder whether Milton had made the whole thing up. I learned later that my biggest handicap was my own pronunciation. You can say over and over to a Cree the name of one of his relatives and he will not recognize it if you have twisted it even a little. I spent some time near Sturgeon River with old Jo Daniels, the wise man of his reserve, repeating to him the names of Milton's Cree and showing him the drawings in the book, none of which he recognized, and it was only later after talking with others that I discovered he was the grandson of Misquapamayoo, Keenamontiayoo's boy. I may as well have been saying the name in Gaelic for all the sense it made to him.

La Belle Prairie, according to Cheadle's diary, was roughly half a mile south of the Crooked River. This presented a problem as there is no Crooked River within a hundred miles of Shell Lake. I took the other clues – a lakeside site, close to the Carlton Trail – and followed the trail up from Shell Lake and enlisted in my hunt everyone living near this route. It all came together on a wooded promontory on the shore of Morin Lake, formerly Devil's Lake. Close to the lake are meadows surrounded by low hills with smaller lakes among the meadows. Roughly half a mile north of this the trail crosses the Big River. On the map the Big River looks like the cardiogram of a hyperactive heart; it is extremely crooked. This was too great a coincidence, and I assumed that either the name had been changed or Milton and Cheadle had assigned their own name to it just as they had La Belle Prairie.

Devil's Lake is a fine spot for a cabin, with the sunsets over the water, and while Milton's has long since rotted away there are holiday homes along the shore where it must have stood. The place looks civilized now, though the winters are still mean. Among the private plots edging the lake on just about the spot where I imagined Fort Milton to have been is a patch of public land that gives access to the lake and on which anybody can do anything. Who or what is conspiring to bring me such luck? There I pitched my tent. There I boiled my plum pudding and watched a sunset bleed over the lake and a low late moon. There I dreamt of Milton and Cheadle dancing dressed as Indians around a large cheese. A dream the significance of which the Cree would no doubt indulge me.

☼

Sam Joseph is one of Keenamontiayoo's great-grandsons. He lives on the Big River reserve near White Fish Lake within a mile of where his ancestor lived during the winter of 1862–63. Despite this it was well into the summer before I found him – the manager of a local store whose wife was a teacher recognized the name from one of her textbooks. Sam signs his name Keenamontiayoo, but everyone knows him by the name given his family by the Christian missionaries who "civilized" them a hundred years or so ago. No one knows Keenamontiayoo. Everyone knows Sam Joseph.

He is in his seventies, about five feet ten, thin with a long face. He wears a baseball cap and jeans held with a smart leather belt and brass clasp. His home is a wooden bungalow in the middle of bush far out on the reserve, and he is the patriarch of a large family, most of whom live there with him. The two things he does not like about modern life are young people's inability to do things for themselves – "people have everything done for them; they can't even build their own houses" – and the mixing of Cree blood with European. He is a proud old-timer and even though he knows little about Keenamontiayoo he has his ancestor's instinct for self-sufficiency. Safest is the man who cuts his own path. His home like all the homes on the reserve has electricity and running water, yet he chooses to sleep with his wife in a separate cabin – which he built himself – that has none. He is one of the few among his people possessing the necessary spiritual attributes – usually signalled in dreams – for conducting the ceremonial festival of renewal and supplication for rain known as a sun dance, and he flies a blue flag over his hut to indicate this. I asked him about my dream of Milton and the cheese, but he said he found it a little too confusing to draw any definite conclusions.

Sam speaks Cree to his son, Barry, who speaks it to his own children. Barry is twenty-seven, has been married for seven years and has three daughters and a son. You get the feeling that this family is Cree before it is Canadian. They are twenty-first-century Cree. They embrace some old ways and some new. Barry goes round-dancing as enthusiastically as he goes to discos. His daughters want to be Spice Girls, but they watch films in Cree. Pinned to the wall in the sitting room is a Traditional Indian Code of Ethics: *Respect the wisdom of people in council. Once you give an idea it no longer belongs to you, it belongs to everybody / Listen to and follow the guidance given to your heart. Expect guidance to come in many forms: in prayer; in dreams; in solitude and in the words and actions of Elders and friends / Receive strangers and outsiders kindly.*

They were all rather astonished that I had come from England to find them. Sam wanted to know how I got there. Did I drive the whole way and how long did it take? He gave me a present for coming – a polyester and nylon blanket imprinted with pictures of timber wolves – but he seemed suspicious of me. I blamed Milton. One look at *The North-West Passage by Land* must have convinced Sam that Milton had single-handedly engineered the demise of the Cree. It may have been the fire-water. Several times he made a thing of telling me that drink had ruined several of his family and he hadn't touched a drop for thirty-five years.

Barry doesn't drink either but he does like to smoke. We shared a smoke and discussed distributor caps. Barry is keen on cars. I told him our great-great-grandfathers had done a nineteenth-century version of this together many times and on almost the same spot, sharing a pipe over things that interested them. Here was a seminal moment. We pondered it, reckoned that if the petrol engine had been around in 1863 then Milton and Keenamontiayoo would probably have discussed distributor caps too.

I said that it would be a fine thing for Barry and me to go hunting together. He thought about it for a few moments and then he said: "I have been known to hunt, but I cannot imagine doing it after a smoke." I agreed it was unlikely to be very productive then but suggested we tried it another time. He fetched his rifle, which established that it was unlikely to be productive at any time. It was a .22 held together with tape with a rusting barrel and battered stock and it looked as if it had belonged to his great-great-grandfather. I doubted its capacity to kill a rabbit. It was not a gun for killing deer, though Barry assured me a friend of his had killed a moose with a .22. "It took ten shots about its body to bring it down but he got it eventually." Keenamontiayoo would not have called that hunting, and neither would Milton. To avoid insulting their memory we agreed it would be better to forget the hunting thing and just talk about it instead.

Of all the rights won by the Natives from the Canadian government when the tribes were settled near the end of the nineteenth century, the right to hunt across their reserves and at any time is one of those held most sacred by the Cree.

At Milton's time they lived to eat, and there was no life without hunting. To uphold the art today is a salute to ancestry and continuity and for some Cree it is more than that, it is almost a spiritual necessity. You can also make money from it and feed your family in the same way you could then, though now you can as well survive without it, and for Barry's generation it does not seem to be a priority.

Barry's uncle George Joseph, another of Keenamontiayoo's great-grandsons, would survive in the body without hunting but he would not survive in the spirit. He still eats everything he kills, for that is the Indian way. I found him on the floor of his kitchen stripping meat from the carcass of a moose, and there were strips of moose meat smoking on a fire in the garden and the smell of game meat everywhere. Keenamontiayoo was a great hunter, said George, and from him comes his own skill and from him his understanding of deer: the tracking and the close-up stalk and the stillness as you pull the trigger in the few seconds you have before the moose gets wise. Think like the animal if you want to take him for he is bigger and better than you. A moose can smell a cigarette from two miles and beside a moose a man is deaf. You need all the luck, a pair of soft deer-hide moccasin-boots for feeling your way through the woods, and a rifle you know well. George knows his rifle well; he has had it for fifty years. It is altogether a different thing to Barry's: a .303 with a magazine and a bolt-action as smooth now as when it was made. There is a spot below the hump on a moose that you need to hit to kill it in one shot, and that is a spot George sees in his sleep.

There was a time during the 1940s when the Cree went back to hunting to survive in the body. They were lean times for everyone in Canada and hunting was banned even for Indians but they risked the punishment for they needed to eat. David LaChance risked six months in prison for a moose (his neighbour got three months for killing a duck). Like Sam Joseph, David LaChance is in his early seventies, one of the wise men of the Big River reserve and for sixteen years was a band councillor. He has a friendly face and wise eyes. When people put their trust in him they are in good hands. He learnt his hunting from "Big Barney" Lacendre, hunter among hunters, trapper among trappers, known to have hammered nails into trees by firing bullets at them. Like George Joseph, David LaChance hunts with his heart: "The thing that makes a good hunter is respect for the animal you are hunting. That is what hunting is about. Many young people today do not have it. They see five elk and they want to kill five. That is not right. I gave hell to a guy who drove up here the other day and ran over two prairie chickens and gave them to me saying I could give them to my dogs. I gave him hell because I drive down that track several times a day past those prairie chickens and every time I slow down for them." This is the wisdom of hunting that Keenamontiayoo imparted to Milton and that I like to think he took to heart, though since he was often short of food on his journey it is hard to judge him on this.

The story of David LaChance's upbringing and of his family is in microcosm the story of the Cree nation since Milton's visit. It is tragedy upon tragedy, each in its way triggered by changes not of the Crees' choosing. David's father died when he was a child. His mother over the course of her childbearing years had twenty-one miscarriages, still-births or babies who lived for only a few hours or days. The doctors put it down to malnutrition. When there was no money at home David trapped rabbits and sold the skins at 50 cents a piece, or muskrat skins at $5. He went out to work on the roads and then he worked on a farm in Alberta, any-thing to feed himself. Since he returned to the reserve he has lost two of his half-sisters, one killed by a car, the other mur-dered. His brother died in an allegedly racist attack in downtown Prince Albert. He has lost two of his sons, one in a car crash and one frozen to death, and both of their deaths were alcohol-related.

Alcohol is banned from sale on the reserves as a result of a clause written into the treaties that the Canadian govern-ment signed with the Indian chiefs and headmen. Among these leaders was Keenamontiayoo, who delayed signing on behalf of his band until 1878 when he was sure the no-alcohol condition would hold. The evil effects of Milton's fire-water must eventually have sunk in. Judging by the pas-sages in *The North-West Passage by Land* describing Keenamontiayoo's character transformation under the influence of rum, he should have been aware for some time that this was not good medicine:

Keenamontiayoo was by this time beyond the reach of argument or reason. . . . Tin cup in hand, he went from one to the other, marking with his finger on the mug the quantity with which he would be content. We firmly refused to give a drop, and as he found we were obstinate, and perceived his chance of succeeding become less and less, his finger descended until at last he vowed that he would be satisfied with the veriest film of liquor which would cover the bottom of the cup. . . . Cheadle at last rather warmly upbraided him with his want of rectitude, when in a moment he drew his knife from his belt, and seizing Cheadle by the collar, pressed the point of the knife against his breast, exclaiming, "Ah! if I were an Indian of the Plains now, I should stab you to the heart if you dared to say no."

He backed down when Cheadle reminded him that he was an Indian of the Woods, who knew better than to resort to violence over a drop of rum. But his behaviour was apparently not unusual alongside that of other Indians faced with prohibition. Milton recalls a band of three hundred Assiniboines turning up at Fort Carlton in full ceremonial dress and war paint, their first visit there for ten years, after two of their tribe on an earlier visit had smelled some rum that had spilled from Milton's cask. They turned out every corner of the fort in search of it, and "failing to discover anything, they expressed great regret that the good news was not true, and requested Mr Lillie [the factor] to forward a strong remonstrance from them to Her Gracious Majesty Queen Victoria, for prohibiting that which her Red Children loved so well, intimating that they themselves were the best judges of what was good for them."

Although alcohol is banned from sale on reserves, it is easy to acquire. Most of the customers at the Native bar at Mount Nebo, east of Shell Lake and off-reserve, appear to be drunk by 10:30 p.m. Some of those who cannot afford to go to a bar simply drink watered-down disinfectant. Why some indigenous peoples should succumb so severely to the effects of alcohol, whether it exploits a genetic fallibility or is some reaction to a new social order, is not clear. It is clear, though, what it has done to them: half the prisoners in Saskatchewan jails are Indian, almost all of whom committed their crimes while drunk or drugged.

I became uncomfortably aware the longer I spent with the Cree and the more stories I heard of alcohol-induced tragedy that, as a white man who had carried rum to their ancestors, Milton was heavily in the dock. All were too polite to mention it, and I was shown no resentment, but it struck me that no one on the Big River reserve had particularly good reason to welcome a descendant of the Great Golden Chief. Perhaps it was fortunate that none of them, not even Sam or George Joseph, knew too much about Keenamontiayoo's life, especially his fraternizing with a buffalo-killing, rum-trading Yorkshireman. On the other hand, if they had known the other sides to Milton they surely would have liked him. He was a champion of their race and he had learnt their language. He had even had a relationship with one of their women (though it is arguable whether this counts in his favour). One gentleman at Big River suggested my dream with the cheese could have only one explanation: that I had Cree blood in my veins and I had returned to the source of it. If only my grandmother had been around to hear that one.

⚹

You cannot blame all the problems on alcohol. The real story of how Cree lives changed after Milton's time is in the Europeans' efforts to divest them of their Cree-ness.

Already by the 1860s the Woods Cree, like all North American Indian peoples, were not what they had been. They had blankets, beads, knives and guns. They had a taste for tea. They had exposure to diseases against which they had no immunity. An epidemic of smallpox in 1781 killed at least half the tribe. By the 1870s there were very few buffalo and Indians everywhere were starving, and this more than anything impelled their leaders to sign the treaties that still define their relationship with the government. The treaty signed by most of the Cree around Fort Carlton in 1876, and by Keenamontiayoo's band in 1878, assigned forever to the British Crown all the "rights, titles and privileges" to the land on which they hunted – amounting to 121,000 square miles, approximately a quarter of today's Saskatchewan and Alberta. In return, the Cree bands were housed on "reserves" of an area equivalent to one square mile for each family of five. They received a one-off payment of $12 each and the promise of an annual payment thereafter of $5, annual supplies of ammunition and twine for fishing nets, fully maintained schools, tools and machinery for farming (four hoes per family, one plough for every three families, a chest of carpenter's tools and four oxen, one bull and six cows for each band, etc.), hunting and fishing rights on the reserves, and a ban on liquor.

Many Cree today say their ancestors did not understand what they were getting into. Few chiefs could read or write English and they could only sign their names with a cross. But the real problem was cultural. The Cree knew nothing of "ownership." They did not see themselves as owning the land on which they hunted and so the idea of surrendering it forever was almost impossible to grasp. Secondly, Cree people are particularly likely to avoid confrontation. They will often answer questions in a way that foremost does not cause offence and that as a result obscures the truth. The truth comes out, but indirectly. Thus a chief or a Canadian government official could claim consensus among Cree who had simply been too polite to vote "no." Similarly, perhaps because of their ceaseless wandering, they never recognized authority in the way Western societies and many other Native groups did. A Cree chief was not a chief in the political sense but through his expertise in a certain area. Big Bear, a Plains Cree, was recognized for his peace-keeping, and the moment his men opened fire at the Frog Lake massacre during Riel's rebellion in 1885 he lost all authority and retreated to his tepee. Keenamontiayoo was recognized for his hunting. It was no coincidence that Keenamontiayoo became a headman, and then a band leader, at the time of the treaty negotiations. The rest of the band appreciated that through his hunting he had gained considerable experience of the white man. (Here was another of Milton's unwitting contributions to the future of these Natives.)

This flexible system of governance is the reason so much Cree culture has survived on the Big River reserve and elsewhere. It has been carried through periods of massive change by many people, rather than being dependent on the survival of just a few. But in dealing with the white man, the Crees' inclination to avoid confrontation put them at some disadvantage, made worse by the language barrier. Today all Cree speak English but few of the white Canadians they deal with have reciprocated. They do not need to, but it can work against them. A story goes that Jean Chrétien, when Minister for Indian Affairs, was giving a speech on a Cree reserve when the crowd started shouting "*moosetoosemay*," a Cree word that Chrétien did not understand. Since the people were also waving their arms and cheering, his officials presumed it was a term of appreciation and advised him to carry on. After the speech, Chrétien was taken to see a farm on the reserve. When he reached a pen of domesticated moose the Cree chief, observing the floor covered in droppings, tapped him on the shoulder and advised: "Watch out, don't step in the *moosetoosemay*." Usually, however, where the whites have not learnt Cree it is the Cree who have lost out.

Once they were fixed to the land, all the government had to do then was fix their minds. This may not have been the way the Europeans went about it but it is the way the Cree see it. The treaty was there to control them and ensure they could not compete. The relationship was paternalistic and dependent, never equalitarian. "Our voice never carried very far," wrote Joseph Dion, a Cree leader from the Kehiwin reserve in northeast Alberta who lived from 1888 to 1960 and whose work was published in 1979 as *My Tribe the Crees*. "We could never appeal direct to the Great White Mother, whose representative at the signing of the treaties had promised to do so much for us. Our Big Brother at Ottawa did not seem to care much, or possibly he was never properly alerted to the plight of the poor wards and the conditions which prevailed in the reserves."

But when it came to fixing minds it was the missionaries rather than the government who were most effective. Milton, a solid Anglican, appears to have had considerable respect for the Crees' nature-spirituality and belief in a creator Father, and he never once implied that they might have done better to worship a Christian God. Indeed, when the evangelical journal *Mission Life*, which also went by the title *The Emigrant and the Heathen*, reviewed his book in 1866 it grumbled: "We are sorry to say that throughout the book the only allusion to the efforts for the introduction of Christianity into the countries described is an account of a Romish Mission Station. An unfavourable impression of Protestant Missions . . . seems to have been created." But Milton's was a generous attitude among whites at the time. The prevailing view of the native religion was rather more uncompromising, as articulated by Hudson's Bay Company employee Robert Ballantyne:

The Supreme Being among the Indians is called the Manitow; but he can scarcely be said to be worshipped by them, and the few ideas they have of his attributes are imperfect and erroneous. Indeed, no religious rites exist among them, unless the unmeaning mummery of the medicine tent can be looked upon as such. Of late years, however, missionaries, both of the Church of England and the Wesleyans, have exerted themselves to spread the Christian religion among these tribes, than whom few savages can be more unenlightened or morally degraded; and there is reason to believe that the light of the gospel is now beginning to shine upon them with beneficial influence. (*Hudson's Bay*, Robert Ballantyne, 1848)

By the 1860s, missionizing had become a competitive business. Rivalry between Anglicans, Catholics and Methodists was sometimes absurdly intense. At Edmonton a month after leaving La Belle Prairie Milton and Cheadle met Father Lacombe, whom they found "exceedingly intelligent" and fluent in Cree. Father Lacombe was benevolent and reasonable, he had spent much time living among the Cree and he was by far the most popular missionary among them at that time. On one occasion, however, he clashed with a Methodist preacher called Reverend Wolsey over the soul of a new convert, an encounter Cheadle recorded in his diary: "Lacombe catches a convert & baptises him. Wolsey hears of it & baptises him over again, & so on ad infinitum, it being with great difficulty that convert knows whether he was made Papist or Protestant last."

The Black Robes, as the preachers were known, had their work cut out. One missionary was delighted to see his

Indian flock enraptured by the story of the Crucifixion, less delighted when they applauded it as an ingenious form of torture and begged him for a diagram showing how it was done. The missionaries had an easier time of it once the Indians were settled on reserves. They ran many of the residential schools to which the Cree were obliged to send their children. There the children had drummed out of them any inclination to practise their native religion and culture – they were punished for speaking Cree or growing their hair long. Yet on the Big River reserve and on many other Cree reserves, the sun dances, round dances and healing sweat lodges persist, alongside Christianity. During prayers in the Catholic Church at Big River the nuns burn sweet grass, traditionally used when praying to the Manitou – an accommodation that would have been unthinkable a century ago.

James Settee is a Cree Anglican preacher who lives near Christopher Lake fifty miles east of Big River in a shoebox house without running water, electricity or telephone but sufficient, he says, for his needs. He is ninety. He has ministered in Big River and all the reserves in the area, he is a good friend of David LaChance and he is popular everywhere because of his compassion and because still he never turns down a baptism, marriage or funeral. The first thing he did when I came into his house was to give me his cup of tea. No time to make another and hope I didn't mind for he was off to the funeral of an infant who had lived for just five hours. James Settee is tall and dignified, he has white hair and high cheekbones and he is all peace and light. He has a story or two. There's the one told by his father of the day he visited the five-hundred-tepee camp of the Sioux band led by chief Sitting Bull, who fled to Saskatchewan after massacring General Custer's regiment at the Battle of Little Bighorn in 1876. His father noticed, behind the Sioux leader at whose feet he was sitting, the scalps of those American soldiers strung from the side of the tepee like a display in a hairdresser's salon, all styles, colours and tints catered for.

James's great-grandfather was a Cree who at the age of six was taken to the Anglican missionary school at Red River. He then became a missionary teacher, and once baptized 107 Indians at one sitting. For this and other successes he was ordained at Red River in 1853, only the second Native to be ordained in the Church of England. The geologist Henry Youle Hind, while surveying the prairies in 1858 for possibilities of settlement, attended a service taken by him at the Qu'Appelle Mission: "The Rev. Mr Settee read the prayers in English with great ease and correctness; he preached in Ojibway, and a hymn was sung in the Cree language."

James's father was born at Fort Garry five years after Milton passed through and later travelled up the Carlton Trail to White Fish Lake the same as Milton. James's father, his grandfather and his brother were all preachers, and now his grandson is thinking of following them. He has an 1850s bible that belonged to his great-grandfather, and imprinted in its opening pages are the rites of passage of all the Settees through whose hands it has passed on its mission voyages across the West: attestation to the Word of God like the tablets of Moses, and James still preaches from it.

Whether or not you approve of missionizing, you have to admire the missionaries' persistence. The Cree are now a predominantly Christian nation, yet not dogmatically so. In accordance with the religious tolerance around these parts, at one church that James Settee visits the children go to a sweat lodge across the road while he preaches to their parents. His great-grandfather would have approved.

In these ways has Cree culture embraced change. In others, however, it seems impervious to it. The Indian treaties stand today much as when they were drawn up – in some respects literally so. Around Big River, the annual individual payments of $5 are still handed out in cash to each person from large boxes brought onto the reserves by government officials and the Royal Canadian Mounted Police. This ceremony is highly uneconomic but for the Natives it is deeply symbolic, and all attempts to change it have failed.

In line with the treaty the Cree, like all Natives, receive free education, housing and welfare, and they pay no taxes. The government may be meeting the terms of the treaty on paper but David LaChance and others say they are not meeting them in spirit. "We receive all this free education and welfare, but at the end of it there are no jobs for us, and no incentives for the young. It is too easy for people just to hang around on the reserves and not work. And when the government hands over money to the band chief it washes its hands of it and gives no guidance as to how it might be spent. A good chief might spend it usefully, a bad one disastrously." Like others, he blames more than a hundred years of colonial rule for a passive Native mindset when it comes to finance – just because the government doesn't say you can do something with the money, they think it means you can't. Until fairly recently, an Indian needed permission to leave his reserve overnight, he could not vote and he could not buy a drink in a bar. Little wonder that freedom, which once defined the Cree, is today a difficult concept for them to grasp.

By the middle of summer I had tied up all the ends from Milton's Indian winter except for one, and this I tied up with the help of a genealogist in Saskatoon who knows the family histories of the Cree better than they know them themselves. He knows who is related to whom across all the reserves and when the blood was mixed. He also knows the great-great-granddaughter of Louis La Ronde, Milton's friend and guide.

She is a compassionate, merry, middle-aged former nurse called Rose Atimayoo who lives in Saskatoon with her son Earlin. She seemed almost as delighted to meet me as I was to meet her. She insisted on coming up to Devil's Lake where she was brought up – Louis, apparently, had returned to Red River after leaving Milton but had been so impressed with the northern prairies that he had gone back there to live. Devil's Lake takes its modern name – Morin's Lake – from the man who married Louis's granddaughter (Rose's grandmother) Judith. Rose had not been back for thirty years and she brought Earlin and her ex-fisherman brother,

Bronco, who had not been back for forty-eight years. They were astonished at how it had all changed – houses fallen, houses built, trees doubled in height. Her parents' log cabin is still there but she does not remember Fort Milton, which untreated and unattended would have rotted away years before. We went to the broken old village on the northern shore where Rose and Bronco had gone to school, and they reconstructed through undulations in the territory, non-portable rocks and the course of a creek the lie of the place as it was then. The only evidence of lives lived on this land are the weathered timbers of the village store, with the cellar that Rose never knew it had exposed in dead-beat resignation to the inconstancy of all things. Bronco remembers playing cards with his mother in front of that store against a husband-and-wife team that fancied themselves a trick or two, and he remembers beating them, and the wife rising indignant from the table and punching her husband hard in the stomach for making her look such a fool.

Memories hardened and immutable. Rose enlisted me to pick rhubarb from the flats a short way down the creek, this rhubarb the sole vestige of a garden once tended by her mother. By the garden there used to be a house, vestiges of which there are none. "Nothing and no one is spared though no death is deserved and there is no telling who will be next," said Rose suddenly, transformed in the middle of her mother's rhubarb to philosopher-reminiscent. All this revisiting was getting to her. But she was happy enough to tell me what she knew of her great-great-grandfather Louis, which mainly concerned his philandering. "There were a whole lot of goings-on in those days, comings and goings, up to no good the lot of them." She'd lost count of the number of wives and mistresses Louis had had. Certainly Paul, the son through whom Rose is descended, was not born of Louis's wife. Rose was smiling and her eyes were all alight and I suggested that she might be prouder of that part of her family history than she was letting on. "Baloney!" she cried. I told her that Milton shared with Louis a similar weakness. "Well then," she said. "That explains everything. It must all have been his fault." Cheeky smile unaltered, sparkling eyes the same.

The path to old age is known by the Cree as the "sweet-grass trail." It is a hard trail fraught with obstacles but all of them surmountable with some luck and the right spiritual help. It was followed successfully by Keenamontiayoo, who lived until 1906 or 1907, and by Louis La Ronde, who was old when he died in the woods near Winnipeg on a trapping expedition. Both of them outlived Milton. Milton's sweet-grass trail is hard to trace and some of the obstacles on it did seem insurmountable. Where his path ran straightest was saddled up under the big prairie sky, or in the woods of the North Saskatchewan running trap-lines with the Cree. Where it ran askew was in England. Here his path became his father's. Whoever's star Milton was born under it wasn't his own.

I often wondered during my time at La Belle Prairie in what ways, if any, I was like Milton. The thought that I always came back to was this: we were both drawn to the wild open spaces. This was why I had followed him out here, it was what had held me transfixed at my grandmother's stories and it was the basis of my affinity for him. How similar we were in character seemed irrelevant. This yearning for a liberation in nature started for me almost on my first day at boarding school, which felt like a prison sentence. I could not imagine when it had started for him. His epilepsy began when he was very young, and so too, I imagined, the social prison sentence that went with it. I had lived my dream of freedom so often in my imagination. The only thing that bothered me was that I had needed Milton as an excuse to experience it for real.

COWBOYS AND INDIANS

They came down out of the woods for the last time on Easter Day 1863 with the ice breaking up on the rivers and too far gone in places to hold them, and they rode down to Fort Carlton with geese on the wing and their domesticity of the past five months disassembled and fetched up into carts. At Carlton they bade goodbye to La Ronde, who according to Milton "positively refused at any price to accompany us further." Perhaps the Rockies were not his territory, perhaps he had had his fill of Englishmen. They also left Rover, who would go with La Ronde to Fort Garry from where they hoped eventually to retrieve him so that he might "spend the rest of his days with his old masters in the ease and comfortable retirement which he earned so well by the faithful and affectionate service he rendered." It was not to be. He died an "untimely death" before they could get him out.

They had planned to spend a day at Fort Carlton before moving on towards the Rockies but they had to stay three because Milton had so much packing and arranging to do. He was an accomplished collector of anything Indian; his bill from the fort was three times Cheadle's. Indian shirts, moccasins, rugs, cloaks. Tools and contraptions. You never knew when you might need them. Cheadle preferred to travel light, and quickly. This was not Milton's way. Milton would never move off in the morning without lighting a fire and cooking breakfast. He would never travel so late that he could not make camp in daylight and he would not go far at all without breaking to assess things, marshal thoughts and energies, light a fire. He loved to light fires. The skill of a fire is in the construction and he must have enjoyed the challenge of that. He built them and lit them wherever he could. Once he set the prairie on fire, another time the forest. Campfires so healthy they must propagate, colonize the unburnt. Shipwrecked on a mud flat on the Fraser River in British Columbia later that year on his way back from the goldfields with some miners he would light a fire in a snowstorm where the rest of the party had failed, an achievement that made it into *The Colonist* newspaper in Victoria: "His Lordship proceeded to cook the evening meal and serve it round to his cold and hungry comrades with an aptitude and grace which surprised and pleased all." Cheadle liked fires but not the way Milton did, and their methods of travel were so different – the one relentless, the other ruminative

– that it's a wonder they got anywhere. Cheadle's frustration is never far from the surface in his diary. "Will Milton never learn the value of time?" His entry for May 27, at Fort Edmonton, is typical of many: "Arguing with Milton all day about taking a tent or a lodge, I voting strongly in favour of the former on account of lightness & small size, he for the latter because most comfortable."

Milton was worst in the mornings and sometimes he flat refused to get up, which incensed his companion, booted and spurred and sharp-set for progress. He must wait for "MiLord." Milton could not designate his morning apathy an epileptic trait before Cheadle, but it was a disposition he had always carried. His tutor Mr. Upton on holiday one summer with the Fitzwilliam children reported to Earl Fitzwilliam that while Milton had managed to walk fourteen miles to the top of a hill and back before lunch he had "not yet been able to make his appearance at breakfast." He added: "But I hope he will soon get into better habits." Some chance.

They still had some three hundred miles to ride from Fort Carlton across much of present-day Saskatchewan and Alberta before they would see the Rockies. Heading out over resuscitated prairie land newly broken from the ice and carpeted in blue anemones they were serenaded by ducks and geese passing northbound and so plentiful that the travellers could not sleep for the perpetual whistling of their wings. They met Indians keen to pass advice on the country through which they would soon be travelling, and they were beset by Indian rumour and myth. Tales the truth of which mattered less than the telling:

Many years ago, but within the memory of people still living, an Indian found a piece of native iron in the neighbourhood of Edmonton, which he carried out to the plains, and placed on the top of a hill. Since that time it had regularly increased in size, and was now so large that no man could lift it! The only thing which makes this tale worth mentioning, is that it obtains universal credence amongst the half-breeds. Many of them profess to have seen it, and one man told us he had visited it twice. On the first occasion he lifted it with ease; on the second, several years afterwards, he was utterly unable to move it!

The Indians believed the Iron Stone had protective powers. They believed that so long as it stayed in their territory they would not starve. So when in 1866 the Methodist missionary George McDougall and his helpers loaded the Iron Stone – by then weighing 386 pounds – onto a cart and carried it to a mission one hundred miles north and thence to Ontario, the Indians were displeased. Their medicine men predicted pestilence, war or starvation. Within a few years they had had all three.

Milton and Cheadle heard stories too of events closer at hand. The Plains Cree and the Blackfoot Indians had just declared a truce after years of war, and parties from both sides were crossing the Saskatchewan River to get a rare peacetime look at each other. The Cree and the Blackfoot were traditional foes and they spent more time stealing each other's horses and raiding camps and avenging killings than they did hunting and trapping and trading. Three years earlier, a Cree war party had killed and scalped a Blackfoot chief. Peeved, the Blackfoot killed twenty people in a Cree village near Fort Pitt and the following year, suspecting a multiracial conspiracy, swore further revenge on any Cree, whites or Métis they came across. They took to attacking the fort – situated on the North Saskatchewan River, north of present-day Lloydminster – which made Milton and Cheadle a little uneasy when they stayed there, despite the truce. It didn't look like much of a truce. An Indian came into the fort one day with news that a Cree woman had just been killed in a Blackfoot camp. She had gone there to marry a Blackfoot chief, but when she arrived another chief announced he desired her for himself. A quarrel ensued, and to end the matter one of them stabbed the Cree woman in the heart. A final if extreme solution.

Milton by consequence stayed up all night at Fort Pitt with a revolver at the ready, but he at least managed to appreciate the singular excitement of a Cree–Blackfoot state visit, which could take place only in times of peace and which the Indians observed by dressing to the nines. The Cree went for colour:

> Scarlet leggings and blankets, abundance of ribbons in the cap, if any were worn, or the hair plaited into a long queue behind, and two shorter ones hanging down on each side the face in front, each bound round by coils of bright brass wire; round the eyes a halo of bright vermilion, a streak

down the nose, a patch on each cheek, and a circle round the mouth of the same colour, constituted the most effective toilet of a Cree dandy.

The Blackfoot, for elegance:

Long gowns of buffalo skin, dressed beautifully soft, and dyed with yellow ochre. This was confined at the waist by a broad belt of the same material, thickly studded over with round brass plates, the size of a crown piece, brightly polished. These Indians were very dignified in manner, submitting with great composure to the gaze of an inquisitive crowd of half-breeds and Crees, who looked with eager interest at a race seldom seen by them, except when meeting on the battle-field.

The strangest story told them from the Blackfoot wars was of a Cree who turned up alone and on foot at Fort Benton on the Missouri River. He was closely followed by a posse of mounted Blackfoot, who on hearing of the enemy within demanded that he be handed over to them for torture and scalping. The chief trader, unwilling to sacrifice the man but equally unwilling to incur the wrath of the Blackfoot, arranged a compromise: they would leave the Cree at the fort for a month, after which time they would return and he would be turned loose with a hundred-yard head start, the Blackfoot bound to pursue him on foot and with no weapons but their knives. When the posse departed the chief trader put the Cree into training, making him run around the fort's enclosure for two hours every day and feeding him on as much fresh buffalo meat as he could take. After a month the Blackfoot returned and the contest began:

> The Cree was placed at his post, 100 yards ahead of his bloodthirsty enemies, who were eager as wolves for their prey. The word was given, and away darted the hunted Indian, the pursuers following with frantic yells. At first the pack of Blackfeet gained rapidly, for terror seemed to paralyse the limbs of the unfortunate Cree, and his escape seemed hopeless. But as his enemies came within a few yards of him, he recovered his presence of mind, shook himself together, his training and fine condition began to tell, and, to their astonishment and chagrin, he left them with ease at every stride. In another mile he was far in advance, and pulling up for an instant, shook his fist triumphantly at his baffled pursuers, and then quickly ran out of sight. He eventually succeeded in rejoining the rest of his tribe in safety.

I did not have warring tribes to worry about but I did have the wind. In the Thickwood Hills west of Fort Carlton it possessed my tent and drew it into ghoulish shapes and it would have drawn it from the ground had I not been inside. It was gusty but behind the gusts was a full-on wind that blew from the south unremitting and bullying like a wind churned from a great engine and there was no hiding from it. I packed up and went down to the road so angled into it I might have been carrying twice the load. Bended trees, hastening tumbleweeds. The erratic paths of birds. Farmed buffalo stood leviathan into the wind and framed against the prairie in a configuration not seen since Milton's time.

I was fixed on the Rockies and getting into the woods out of the wind, as soon as I could get a lift westwards. Most of that day I sat by a road on which travelled few vehicles and none of them stopping and none likely to. The Cree who picked me up in the late afternoon was on his way back to his reserve and he said people didn't stop in a wind for fear of dust. I told him it seemed a lame reason and he agreed, and then he said maybe it was less a fear of dust than of the lunacy apparent in those out walking in such a wind. He dropped me north of the town of Paradise Hill and I got another lift into the town. The Métis who drove me in and to whom I told my story said he knew someone in that town whom I really should meet, and he delivered me to the door of Dan Palsich's house as if delivering a lost animal to a vet. Dan would know what to do.

His house, which he built himself, is on the Carlton Trail, a significance not lost on him. Since living there he has become a Carlton Trail specialist and knows all who travelled on it and their accomplishments. He knows about Milton. He has read Milton's book. He has immortalized him with Cheadle and other Carlton Trail heroes on a large signboard that stands beside the road at the head of the town. Thus, as he told all his friends later, he took some time to calm down after finding Milton's great-great-grandson looking shifty and uncertain on his doorstep. An apocryphal deliverance. I said it worked both ways since it was uncommon for me to find someone who knew Milton's book. And there was yet more significance. Dan's wife Alba, who is blind, used to work as a teacher on the Big River reserve, and she named people, some of whom I knew, and she asked for news of them. Fibres of life entwined, all roads lead into one. Alba has been blind for six years and there is only one thing in their house she has not seen: a large painting of the Carlton Trail through Paradise Hill as it would have looked one hundred years ago. It depicts homesteads and travellers and wooden Red River carts that were the freight traffic of the prairies and whose approach was heralded by a symphonic squeaking from unlubricated wheels. Dan bought this painting and he is proud of it, and it is a difficult thing for them that Alba has never seen it. They gave me supper and insisted I stay the night. They had known me for two hours and I had turned up unannounced and in the dark. Was it even conceivable that this could happen in England?

The next morning Dan took me to "Coffee Row," an assembly of men of the town who gather in a café each morning to discuss the things that need discussing: the weather; their wives; what they did the night before. It looked like the Saskatchewan equivalent of the Coffee Mugs, though I presumed I was safe from hair-ruffling. Here female influences are dispelled. I was introduced. Grunts and nods of approval, silence. One of the men said he knew of Milton, had read Dan's book. More grunts, clattering of coffee mugs, careful consideration of the sickly liquid within. These guys should take a lesson from the Mugs in how to gossip. I could put the two assemblies in touch. Then again, such men of so few words in close contact with matrons so spirited could be rendered mute forever. I decided to spare them.

After a few coffees conversation warmed up. Fred, a geologist friend of Dan, talked of his days in the Yukon in the 1960s and 1970s and the old miners there known only by their nicknames Home-Brew John, Cucumber Pete, Bombay Peggy. Bombay Peggy was in fact not a miner but a cultured English "remittance-lady" whose erratic ways did not suit her well-to-do English family and who was thus sent off to India. But she ended up in Dawson Creek in the Yukon where she ran a brothel and sold alcohol to the miners. I said that black sheep in well-to-do English families were not thin on the ground. No one could say why so many ended up in Canada but Fred maintained Canada had plenty of home-grown eccentrics. An old boy from this town once kept two young beavers as pets just like Grey Owl, the Englishman who moved to Saskatchewan in the early twentieth century and became an outspoken conservationist and an Indian in all but blood. These beavers would follow the fellow everywhere, they would sit on bar stools next to him and sip beer. One day he left them at home and when he got back he found all his furniture chewed, legs eaten off tables and chairs. The beavers had teethed. This was the last thing they did as pets.

As is the way in the countryside, Dan later that day passed

me on to someone else. He chose Edgar Mapletoft, seventy-nine-year-old caretaker of the Fort Pitt site, honorary elder of a local Cree Indian band and self-styled tour guide, who seemed more at ease with the nineteenth century than the current one. He drove me out to Fort Pitt in a kind of trance in which we battled for our place on the road with imaginary Red River carts, swerved for imaginary buffalo, saluted groups of imaginary fur-clad Indians. His driving reminded me of my grandmother's. I hoped he could distinguish between real and imaginary trucks. His car, which he treated as the latest all-terrain four-by-four, might have been built when the Carlton Trail was still in use. Every attempt at the indicators set off the windscreen wipers. He used potholes to brake.

"Do you mind me asking where you learnt to drive?" I said.

"Learnt? I don't remember ever learning."

He turned right suddenly onto a dirt track. At least two of the wheels took the curb. Why go the long way round?

"I had a grandmother who would have been impressed with your driving," I said.

"Fantastic. Was this grandmother a descendant of Milton?"

"His granddaughter."

"Fantastic. Sounds like there's some crazy streak down that side of your family then."

I laughed and said it was only crazy if you thought of it that way and that mostly it was just people expressing themselves as best they could and it was those around them that made them look crazy. This Edgar understood, and thank goodness, he said, for such people, for without them the world would be less colourful and life less explored.

✧

Resourceful, English and public-school hardened as they were, Milton and Cheadle were not too proud to concede that they would need help in getting through the mountains to British Columbia. It was one thing to follow a trail over a flat prairie, another to cut your own through forest and cross rivers in spate without maps and without a clue.

So from the Métis at Fort Carlton and Fort Pitt they chose two guides. Baptiste Suprenat, "tall, powerful, and like all his race very talkative," claimed he knew the way to Tête Jaune Cache on the western side of the main Rocky Mountain ridge. They agreed on a fee of £12 a month. He could not have known what he was in for. They do not say much else about him. They do not mention his wife, Katherine Parisien, nor that he married her when she was eleven. That might have been too much for the British public to bear.

As an assistant guide they engaged Louis Patenaude, known as "the Assiniboine" on account of his having been brought up by that tribe. He was

a middle-sized though athletic man, of very Indian appearance. His hair was long and black, and secured by a fillet of silk, his nose prominently aquiline, his mouth small, and with unusually thin and delicate lips. His manner was very mild and pleasing, and the effect of this was increased by the singular softness and melody of his voice.

Through my friend the Saskatoon genealogist I discovered that the Assiniboine's first wife married "Jem" Simpson, illegitimate son of Sir George, the Hudson's Bay Company governor of Rupert's Land. I also discovered that the Assiniboine's descendants and Louis La Ronde's descendants are related through marriage. In such ways at that time were the people of the Canadian West from myriad origins bound together by blood.

When Milton met him at Fort Pitt, the Assiniboine was with his second wife and eleven-year-old daughter, Theresa, who was seriously ill. She died four days later. This tragedy in the life of the man in whose close company they would spend the next five months takes up one sentence in *The North-West Passage by Land* and one sentence in Cheadle's diary, and it is mentioned only in relation to how it would inconvenience their departure. It all sounded a little *insensible* and Victorian.

The Assiniboine's "set-back" did indeed change things. He now insisted that he would go with them only on the condition that he could bring his wife and thirteen-year-old son as well. This was not quite what Milton had in mind, but he was so taken with the fellow that he eventually agreed, albeit not without misgivings. The Assiniboine must have been quite a charmer, since he was further disadvantaged by having only one hand. He had lost the other to a misfiring gun, a detail he persuaded Milton would have no impact whatsoever on his performance. It also emerged that beneath his mild and pleasing manner lay something more passionate: "Although his countenance beamed forth benevolent, and he cooed softly as any dove when at peace, yet, when angry and excited, his aspect became perfectly fiendish, and his voice thundered like the roar of a lion." They would learn several weeks into the Rockies that the Assiniboine had been dismissed from the Hudson's Bay Company for killing a man in a drunken squabble. But they excused him even this, allowing that the dead man had been a notorious bully and "the dread and terror of all the half-breeds." As it turned out their judgement was sound, for the Assiniboine would be their salvation.

At Fort Edmonton, site of today's city, 150 miles west of Fort Pitt and their last port before the mountains, they recruited their fifth, final and most unlikely companion – though it was more a case of Mr. Eugene Francis O'Beirne recruiting them:

> An Irishman of between forty and fifty years of age, he was dressed in a long coat of alpaca, of ecclesiastical cut. . . . He carried an enormous stick, and altogether his appearance showed a curious mixture of the clerical with the rustic. . . . He introduced himself to us with a little oration, flattering both to himself and us, remarking that he was a grandson of the celebrated Bishop O'B., and a graduate of the University of Cambridge; we should readily understand, therefore, how delightful it must be for him, a man of such

descent and education, to meet with two members of his own beloved university so intellectual as ourselves. He informed us that he was a man of peaceful and studious habits, and utterly abhorred the wild and dangerous life to which he was at present unfortunately condemned. He next astonished us by telling us almost as much about our relations, friends, and acquaintances as we knew ourselves; their personal appearance, where they lived, what property they had, their families, expectations, tastes, peculiarities, and his opinion of them generally.

Cheadle in his diary is more candid:

> He is a great talker & I fancy a great humbug & "ne'er do well" who has been a dead weight on his friends throughout. Seems a well-informed fellow, however, & nearly knocked my head off with Latin quotations. Horribly afraid of bears & even wolves. He wishes to go with us, & intimates it will be our interest to take him, which we can't see as he is the most helpless fellow in the world. . . . Poor fellow, I wish we were not so short of carts, or we would willingly give him a lift, although he is an ungrateful dog.

They did give him a lift, to their eternal regret. He is so improbable a character and so delighted and troubled readers of *The North-West Passage by Land* that Milton felt obliged to add to later editions a preface asserting his validity. Fearing he needed to justify his decision to bring on board such an incompetent, he added: "Should Mr O'B. be

the means of drawing attention to and promoting the settlement of the Fertile Belt, and the formation of an Overland
Route to the Pacific across British America, he will have rendered his country very valuable service."

Subsequent authors have confirmed the existence of this
prairie fool, and also made it clear that O'Beirne did not
give Milton his full story. For a start, he was no grandson of
the celebrated Bishop Thomas O'Beirne, whose only son
had died unmarried. He was born around 1810 in Ireland
and attended a Roman Catholic theological college at
Maynooth called St. Patrick's, from which he was expelled
in 1830. Thus insulted, he became an apostate and set off on
an anti-Catholic lecture tour of England, discoursing on the
dangers of that Church and especially of "that den of filth
and iniquity," the College of Maynooth. The *Bradford
Observer* described him as "an individual of doubtful reputation," noting that during one lecture some of his state-
ments were so offensive to his audience that he was made to
stop. He was admitted to St. John's College, Cambridge, in
October 1842, but the following February was persuaded to
move to Clare College, which suffered him for a year and a
half before removing him from its rolls. He withdrew to
India. After a couple of years, with help from an old college
friend, he landed a job as secretary to a wealthy planter in
Louisiana, where he kept out of trouble until the American
Civil War. Imagining somehow that he would be excused
any part in hostilities, he was horrified when he heard he
had been elected Captain of the Home Guard. Here Milton's
portrayal runs true:

The newly-elected captain was horror-struck – visions of sharp-pointed bayonets directed against his abdomen, and keen swords flashing in descent upon his cranium, rose before his mental eye; the roar of cannon and musketry, and the whistle of bullets, seemed already to sound in his affrighted ears; wounds, agony, and death to stare him in the face. Stammering out thanks, less warm than seemed appropriate to the warlike Southerner, he stole away from his disappointed friend, and secretly made preparations for escape.

He made his way north and in 1861 ended up in the Red River Settlement, where according to J. J. Hargrave in *Red River* he became "quite a temporary celebrity" and was known as the "Irish schoolmaster." He found a taste for rum and a reputation as a scrounger: "As his bill at the hotel was getting in arrear, he commenced a round of visits . . . to the houses of such hospitably disposed acquaintances as he had met, reserving the great bulk of his patronage for the clergymen." Inevitably he outstayed his welcome here and was hurried on westwards with a party of miners from the East known as the Overlanders, who were set for the goldfields of British Columbia. From them he earned his greatest obloquy. They noted his

inordinate selfishness, his colossal impudence, his flagrant ingratitude, his unconscionable egotism, and his intolerable indolence. Add to all the above mean qualities that of dishonesty, and you have an accurate, but uninviting, analysis of the insufferable sycophant." (*The Overlanders of '62*, Mark Sweeten Wade, 1931).

They deposited him at Fort Carlton, from where he buffooned his way to Fort Edmonton and that fateful meeting with Milton, alumnus of his old alma mater. He must hardly have believed his luck. What was Milton thinking in asking him along? Afterwards, in a lecture about their journey, he called O'Beirne their most serious impediment, and thoroughly unfit to have ever left his university in England.

Fort Edmonton had a reputation as the most hospitable Hudson's Bay Company outpost in the West. It must have lived up to it, for Milton and Cheadle stayed three weeks. This might have been because Mr. Hardisty, who was in charge, was keen on balls and uncommonly generous with food. His banquets had a uniquely prairie edge: boiled buffalo hump; buffalo rump; venison; buffalo calf, removed from its mother by Caesarean section and boiled whole; dried moose nose, or *mouffle*; whitefish browned in buffalo marrow; beavers' tails; roasted wild goose with potatoes and turnips; prairie chicken; buffalo tongue. You had to like buffalo. People would ride for days for such dainties, though in 1846 the Canadian artist Paul Kane, who was the last tourist before Milton to cross the Rockies through Edmonton, complained a little ungraciously that "no pies, plum puddings, or blanc manges, shed their fragrance over the scene." Food was a soft currency on the prairies. The prize for winning a race at the fort's traditional New Year's Day sports event was generally a "blow-out" of pemmican.

Milton reckoned his reception at Edmonton "did great credit to Mr Hardisty and the hospitaly [sic] of the H.B.C. making a great contrast to the treatment of travelers at some of the other posts on this side of the mountains. . . . Edmonton was one of the only forts I ever left with regret." He was not there solely to indulge himself, however. If they did not buy supplies at Edmonton, fatten their horses and trade for others, garner local knowledge, they would come adrift in the mountains like others before them. Hardisty and his officers tried to make them change their minds about their route to British Columbia on account of the impenetrable forest and unfordable rivers they'd be sure to meet, but they'd made up their minds and would give no quarter to such soft-bellied counselling. They stocked up: two hundred-pound sacks of flour and four ninety-pound bags of pemmican, some tea, salt and tobacco. This to last eight hundred miles to the next fort at Kamloops, which they judged – poorly as it happened – would take them fifty days. Milton swapped a gun for a good horse. They tipped the servants at Edmonton, spent their last farthing. They wrote letters home. Those would be some letters to read, and where are they now, written on that evening of June 2, 1863, their last behind walls for longer than they would have wagered?

Other travellers had gone before them up the Carlton Trail to Fort Edmonton and west through the Yellowhead Pass to Tête Jaune Cache and then down the Fraser River or the North Thompson or the Columbia on the west side of the Rocky Mountains to the coast, but they left few records. Captain John Palliser, commissioned by the British government in 1857 to study the suitability of the prairies for settlement, came up the Carlton Trail and into the mountains, but he crossed them by the Kootenay Pass further south. When his botanist, Dr. Hector, tried to reach the headwaters of the North Thompson, he found the forest and fallen timber too dense to cut through. Henry Youle Hind, who surveyed the prairies after Palliser for the Canadian government and whose book *A Sketch of an Overland Route to British Columbia* Milton and Cheadle carried from the Red River settlement to the coast, also stayed south. Alexander Mackenzie, David Thompson, Simon Fraser and George Simpson sniffed around north and south but never attempted the Yellowhead. Paul Kane painted his way down the Columbia to Fort Vancouver. Milton was fixed on the Yellowhead because it was the only pass that came out near the Cariboo goldfields and thus seemed to him the most useful northwest trading passage by land – and also because it was unmapped and because everyone tried to talk him out it. If he was going to push at boundaries he might as well push them all the way. Try talking Milton out of anything.

The only recorded non-Indian travellers who had gone the whole way across that pass to Tête Jaune Cache and down the North Thompson River or the Fraser were the Overlanders. After ejecting O'Beirne at Fort Carlton in the summer of 1862, this group of emigrants traded carts for pack saddles and rode to the Athabasca and up that river and over the pass to the Cache – 125 men, Catherine Schubert, wife of one of the miners, her daughter and her two sons slung in baskets from their horse, and a milking cow. At the Cache the party split, one group going on rafts and dugout canoes down the Fraser to Fort George, the other down the North Thompson to Kamloops. The day she arrived in Kamloops, Catherine Schubert gave birth to a girl, the first white girl born in the interior of British Columbia.

Several of the Overlanders drowned on the rivers, but Milton and Cheadle in June 1863 did not know this, and neither did they know whether any had made it nor the state of the rivers on which they had travelled. André Cardinal, who had guided the Overlanders to Tête Jaune Cache and the North Thompson group to the main branch of that river, was at Edmonton with Milton and Cheadle. They pressed him for details of the route but they found his answers contradictory and obscure.

Milton had his first taste of what he had taken on in O'Beirne the day before they left the fort. "My Lord, and Dr Cheadle," began the Irishman. "I am sure you will thank me for a communication which will enable you to escape the greatest danger. I have been credibly informed that this 'Assiniboine' is a cold-blooded murderer, a villain of the deepest dye, who has been excommunicated by the priest, and is avoided by the bravest half-breeds. You don't mean to tell me that you really intend to trust your lives with such a man?" They confirmed that they did. "Then in the name of your families," he cried, "I beg to enter my most solemn protest against the folly of such a proceeding. I am firmly convinced that we shall all fall victim to his murdering ways." The Assiniboine for his part was hardly charmed by the thought of accompanying this bumbling ineffectual through some of the toughest country in the West. After he returned to England, Milton would hear from Dr. Rae – whom La Ronde had accompanied in search of Franklin in the early 1850s and who crossed the Yellowhead in the summer of 1864 – a rumour circulating at Edmonton that the Assiniboine had knocked off Milton's entire party and was living well off their horses and possessions. No doubt he had thought about it. In their frustration with O'Beirne, Milton, Cheadle and the Assiniboine resorted to practical jokes, the first while they were still at Edmonton:

> O'Beirne was attacked by a number of ailments which required the Doctor's advice daily. After submitting unflinchingly to active treatment for several days, he at last confessed that his malady was imaginary, and merely assumed as an excuse for obtaining private interviews. But Cheadle maliciously refused to believe it, assured him he was really seriously unwell, and compelled him to swallow a tremendous dose of rhubarb and magnesia.

Into that country of adventurers and gold-seekers this motley crowd set out westwards and mountain-bound. They were observed in silence by the disbelieving inhabitants of Fort Edmonton, who put at long odds their chances of reaching the coast and laid out the many scenarios in which they might fail. They rode out with twelve horses, a guide who knew only half the way, as his assistant a one-handed murderer who had never before been west of

Edmonton, a thirteen-year-old boy and his mother, and a mooncalf abandoned by every traveller who had taken him on. It was an unlikely combination, if survival was what Milton had in mind.

HORSEPLAY

I learnt to ride in England on a horse called Stinker. The people who own Stinker said he was a quiet, kindly animal, used to greenhorns and aspiring more to a life in grass than the extravagant displays of horsiness to which their daughter managed to excite him. Really, they said, he should have been named Dobbin. Soft as a cat.

Sly as a cat more like, and Stinker was just the right name for him. He saw me coming three fields away. A good friend of my father had agreed to teach me all I needed to know about horses in a single weekend in Gloucestershire, capital county for horses. He is a very good horseman but he had not counted on Stinker. Stinker belongs to his neighbours and I reckoned he saw him coming three fields away too; either that or they were in league. That horse seemed a little too pleased to see us, too willing to have me mount up and be led into the paddock, too submissive by half to my infantile manipulation of the reins. He was biding his time, knew for certain if he kept it up that my father's friend would slip the leading rein, knew with even greater certainty who would be in control when he did.

When it happened we were in a large field that ran down from the gate in a bowl to a wood. We went through the gate and my teacher unclipped the lead. I wondered for a moment whether he had also stuck a pin in Stinker's backside, such was the effect it had on this hitherto model of a riding-school tortoise. We descended the hill pursued by an imaginary pack of horse-eating wolves. By the time we reached the bottom I had lost my hat and I had lost the stirrups – not that I had ever really found them – and I could see that Stinker was going for the fence and that that would be a spectacular end to it. Always unpredictable, he instead lurched to the left and embarked on the first of several tight circuits of the bowl before climbing back up the hill to the gate. Spent and steaming like a manure heap, he stamped to a halt beside "the boss" who, transfixed by this circus, had not moved. I was too astounded to speak. Stinker looked triumphant. But he was forgetting something: I was still in the saddle. I felt faintly victorious, though hatless. Milton would have had a thing or two to say, not all of them polite, but he would have enjoyed the rodeo.

It got better. I progressed to a polo stables, mucked out and learnt the dirty side of keeping horses and how to sit in a saddle without stirrups and reins and still have some kind of control. I had my backside scraped raw by an unkind saddle on rough-cut jeans during half an hour of relentless cantering. The grooms found it funny that I could not sit down properly for three days and I did not mind, for I knew all this was breaking me in. A little more time and I'd be set for another go at Stinker.

Len Carroll is seventy-one and he knows a thing or two about horses. He used to work out of Jasper taking hunters into the Rockies after deer and bear and bighorn sheep. He'd be with the horses sleeping out in the mountains, a hundred days at a run and a hundred days more would have been fine with him. He worked horses for film crews who came to shoot Westerns on the snow-melt rivers and he took the part of bad guy or Indian in some of these films, flinging himself from the saddle where no one else would. Films such as *River of No Return* with Robert Mitchum – "he was a tough mean old bugger and no one touched him at the bar" – and Marilyn Monroe, whom Len taught to ride, and *The Far Country* with James Stewart, suitability for all of which depended on how little you cared for your own safety. I had met Len in March in Manitoba where he now lives and I tried to persuade him to return to the Rockies to take me down Milton's trail. Though he said he fancied such a campaign, he was still recovering from an accident in which a horse rolled on him and broke his pelvis. He rode home semi-conscious standing in one stirrup and the horse knew just where to take him. He would call me afterwards in England to check on how things went, always between the hours of two and four in the morning. Time zones never meant much to him.

But Len still knew people who worked horses west of Edmonton and through them I found Dave. They do not come more regular cowboy and fit for the bush than Dave. He spent seven years as a warden in Jasper National Park and worked as an instructor at a search-and-rescue centre for Canadian Air Force pilots, teaching them how to survive on their own with nothing in unfamiliar territory. Now he runs a guiding and outfitting business out of Jasper in western Alberta. He knows about survival in the backcountry and he knows about horses; he owns about a hundred of them. Dave's wife, Chris, used to take hunters into the mountains the way Len did, and they are united by horses and wilderness. In many other ways they are different. Dave chooses words carefully and you have to draw them out of him; he is cautious with words and people and when he speaks it is mostly about the job in hand, the job in hand being what he has in mind most of the time. He likes to get a job done and he does it well. When he laughs you know your joke is funny, though he is never bad-humoured. It is hard to imagine a better person with whom to be in the mountains. Chris is as good as Dave in the mountains but she is open and gregarious and easy with people. She laughs most of the time. She is thirty-two like me and Dave is thirty-eight.

When I told them I wanted to cross the Rocky Mountains the way Milton had done Dave said he'd heard of crazier schemes. I said he'd better wait to see me ride and then he might want to rearrange his list. I asked him how much he would charge to take me for a few weeks and he suggested a sum and it sounded fine. Chris would come too, he said. I told him about Milton's Assiniboine guide who had refused to travel without his family and wondered whether this was the tradition in these parts. Did Dave have a thirteen-year-old son who might like to come too, or indeed a criminal record that might be relevant to our partnership? He smiled and said he was beginning to like this Lord Milton fellow.

To follow Milton faithfully through the Yellowhead Pass to Tête Jaune Cache would mean riding up the Yellowhead Highway. The Canadian government eventually agreed with Milton – decades after his death – that the pass would make a good northwest passage to British Columbia, and the highway follows his route precisely for several hundred miles. Milton had done his job well, but this was no help to me. Riding on a road was hardly an adventure, nor would it show me what he went through. So Dave suggested heading north away from the highway and then west following a trail which, though thirty miles removed from Milton's, was similar to what his would have been like in the 1860s. No one had been up there to change anything – same country, same hardship, same basket of unpredictables. Spend weeks with horses in the Rockies and the travelling will be the same whichever century you choose.

So one day in early September, some forty miles northeast of Jasper off the road from Edmonton, we loaded five packhorses with food and the indispensables of horse-travel and we saddled up a riding horse each and set off into the forest. There was full sunshine though the white spruce trees that dominate these forests are selective with the light they let through and on the cold and silent floor it felt almost funereal. We rode among deadfall twisted and skeletal, the cycle of birth and death laid out in holocaustal shapes. Mushrooms of unknown toxicity, silverberry, ubiquitous feather moss prospering in the dimness and decay. The symbiotic forest. The inclined trunks of trees still living creaked and shifted against each other like the timbers of some forsaken ship. Spruce grouse stared out from the undergrowth. You can pass within four feet of these imprudent sentries and they will not shift.

I rode a roan called Comanche that required "encouragement," such was his predilection for slow walking and grass. Dave rode Flair, the horse that had carried the Marlboro Man in a recent television advertisement and was a cut above. Chris rode Spook. The packhorses were a bull-headed roan named Hector, a paint horse which Chris wanted to call Apache but which answered to Baldy, Whisky-jack, Coal and Poncho. They were an improbable team and they were herded every step by Kellie, Dave's border collie, who could not help her immaculately timed hoof-nips despite outlandish cursing from her master. This would be my family for subsequent weeks and they seemed a well-set bunch next to Milton's crowd.

✿

Soon after leaving Fort Edmonton, Milton and his posse came to the traders' settlement at Lac Ste. Anne and, mindful of privations imminent, popped in for some milk and fish with Colin Fraser. Fraser was the local Hudson's Bay Company officer. He had not been east of Edmonton for fifteen years and for thirty years had not seen Fort Garry and was perfectly content with this. "A very fine old fellow indeed and of Highland hospitality as well as birth," observed Cheadle. He had come to British North America in 1827, aged twenty-two, as Sir George Simpson's private bagpiper. Simpson suffered no weaklings and though he respected Fraser's piping he was less impressed with his state of fitness. During his tour of the area in 1828 he noted: "We are getting on steadily considering the state of the Water & the Weakness of some of our Men. . . . the Piper cannot find sufficient Wind to fill his Bag." Fraser piped the Overlanders on their way and he saw off Milton and Cheadle with a smoke and a fit of storytelling.

They crossed the Pembina River into heavy forest on a path beset with marsh and mosquitoes. They could hold off from their pemmican for now and feast on pigeon and spruce grouse, though these birds offered little sporting challenge, lining up on branches as if waiting to be shot – which they duly were. The travellers shared this country with grizzly bears, which excited Milton and fairly finished O'Beirne:

> Mr O'B. was a man of most marvellous timidity. His fears rendered his life a burden to him. But of all the things he dreaded his particular horror was a grisly bear. He was in the

daily expectation of meeting one of these terrible animals, and a sanguinary and untimely end at the same time. As he walked through the forest, the rustle of every leaf and the creaking of the trunks seemed, to his anxious mind, to herald the approach of his dreaded enemy. The Assiniboine, taking advantage of his weakness, cured him for a time of his carelessness in losing sight of the party, by lying in wait, hid amongst the trees close to the track, and as Mr O'B. passed by, set up a most horrible growling, which caused him to take to his heels incontinently, and for several days he kept near protection.

Even the boy joined in the baiting of "Le Vieux," dressing in a buffalo robe and ghosting about in the outskirts of the firelight. I began to feel a little sorry for Eugene Francis, a fish a long way from water, though this is not a sentiment shared by Milton. It can't have helped him that in this forest the Assiniboine himself was nearly done in by bears when, confronted by three of them, both barrels of his shotgun misfired. Short of options, the Assiniboine stood his ground. The bears, bemused, backed down. Another man might have cut his losses but the Assiniboine retreated, recharged his gun and came up on them from another side, pulling the trigger on two more misfiring barrels. Disbelieving, the bears postured, displayed teeth – and decided to waste no more energy on such an incompetent.

People say it's surprising what you can get away with if you stand your ground in front of a grizzly. A Cree gentleman at La Belle Prairie, when he heard I was set for the

Rockies, had volunteered some advice about grizzly bears, as a great number of people have done starting with my grandmother. This Cree said I'd do well to follow his advice since it was based on his own experience and he was still there to tell me the story. Everything the bear does you do too. If the bear takes five steps forward you take five forward. You bark when the bear barks. All this the Cree does and the bear, who is by then within four yards of him, squats down to shit. The Cree goes through these motions too, though he tells the bear it is really quite unnecessary for he did it in his pants when they first met. Impressed, the bear backs off.

Dave said that people often come to Jasper National Park to test out new ways of repelling bear attacks. The craziest he's heard of is a padded bear-proof suit designed as protection from all bear violence. The inventor took it out in the woods near Banff to test it on the real thing, with marksmen attendant in case it failed, but he hadn't counted on the rough terrain and he found he couldn't walk three yards in it without falling over. Dave reckoned he might have problems selling this to hikers.

They reached the McLeod River. Milton panned for gold, found "good colours." He seemed to know what he was looking for. He also seemed to know where he was going and how he aimed to get there, for when Baptiste suggested alternative ways of travelling, alternative schedules, alternative camping sites, he protested and they quarrelled. A few days later Baptiste disappeared and never returned. He had taken some pemmican, tea, O'Beirne's saddle-bags, their last long-handled axe and one of Milton's horses. This had always been his plan, they surmised. Or perhaps he had decided that survival was unlikely with O'Beirne in the party, or that he had different ideas to Milton and there was no way around him. He would have been right on that one. Milton festered over the horse and formed plans for revenge but they could not go after Baptiste and so they promoted the Assiniboine to position of guide and went on. It made the whole enterprise even more improbable:

> We could not conceal from ourselves that the work would be very heavy. We had thirteen horses to pack and drive through the thick woods; the one-handed Assiniboine, with his wife and boy, were our only assistants; and Mr O'B represented a minus quantity. At least six or perhaps seven hundred miles of the most difficult country in the world lay before us, and not one of the party had ever previously set foot in this region.

Yet there was never the slightest suggestion that they might abandon their plans.

As if to exorcise his anger, Milton the next day set the forest on fire. It was hardly his fault. One of the horses kicked out a burning log from his fire, and it ignited a fallen pine which ignited a stand of pines which being pines and tinder-dry would burn until they were charcoal. They pailed water from a nearby lake and axed down the surrounding trees to contain it, but it was a close-run thing and they nearly lost one of their horses when, insensible with panic, it rolled in the fire. They had to beat it about the head before it would move. For miles as they rode on they watched the smoke rise from the isolated inferno. Fire is a natural part of the forest cycle but this was an unnatural fire. The Royal Geographical Society in London, self-appointed standard-bearer for responsible travel, had Milton remove all references to this incident from his script before allowing him to lecture. It also made him remove every reference to O'Beirne (who needless to say during the fire had sat on a log and relaced his boots). Incompetence, apparently, was the gravest indignity. Real explorers did not fool around. Still, it seemed to work for Milton. He never again mentioned Baptiste.

We climbed through the spruce and we came out of the darkness into meadows and into the heat of the day. The meadows were fed by creeks that run off the Snake Indian River and there was good feed for the horses and it was hard to keep Comanche on the job. Some of the creeks had been dammed by beavers and those industrious animals could now dictate how the creeks should run. They had bitten through whole trees in construction for their waterworlds. The Snake Indian, like most Rocky Mountain rivers, comes out of a glacier and it flows east and then southeast into the Athabasca River north of Jasper, near the site of the old Hudson's Bay Company outpost at Jasper House. The river is named after a small tribe whose members lived in this valley and who were also called the Snaring Indians on account of their adhesion to that hunting method. The Snake Indians were wiped out by a band of Assiniboine that coveted their hunting grounds. A river named in blood it carries the dust of an extinct people. It is a beautiful and lively river for all that.

Turning west up the Snake Indian during that first week we covered two or three miles an hour at a walk and aimed for ten to twenty miles a day, though we would not travel every day. We had deep sit-in saddles and low-slung stirrups and one-handed reining with no pressure at the bit, and what would Stinker have thought of that? We followed a creek northwest off the Snake Indian and made camp in a clearing ringed by spruce. Any place is fine to camp that has running water for us and grass for the horses. We turned out the horses with hobbles on their front legs and bells around their necks and they lurched out of camp towards the grass like crazy and malappropriated circus horses fettered for entertainment. Bells marking the movements of the bonded.

Those lonely silent nights, when thoughts deep-held and troublesome emerge like crystals out of solution. Silence and darkness crowded with noise and imagery. Some nights in those mountains, every longing I'd ever felt seemed to surface for consideration, every insecurity, every girl. You must pay them scant attention for they will stick around. Let them surface and then let them evaporate. Most thoughts you can let go but there's always one you can't. It's always the girl. All the loneliness settles on her.

After leaving La Belle Prairie and before continuing west into the Rockies I had returned to England briefly for my brother's wedding. "Unkempt," suggested my mother as I tried on my ill-fitting morning suit, renewed acquaintance with a hairbrush. "You'll startle the great-aunts." Fortunately my brother, second to getting married, would have loved to have been in the backwoods himself, so quite understood. I wondered if he had fixed up the honeymoon. If not, I knew an ideal spot beside a lake in Saskatchewan; he might even find himself a romantic old cabin. He acknowledged the merit in this idea and received a sharp elbow in the ribs from his fiancée.

My girlfriend had met me at the airport. She was supposed to come to the wedding but she did not, for with grim inevitability things started to go wrong fairly quickly. There is no more suitable Day of Judgement for your girlfriend than the day your younger brother gets married. I think she tried to imagine me in his place and, well, couldn't. I couldn't either. "Back to the woods with you and leave her alone," was the general sentiment among her friends. "Back to the woods with you and forget about it," was the general sentiment among mine.

But you don't just forget about it. Travel to a lonely place when you've started off lonely and that's how to miss your girl. They always follow you out there in your head. There to point out for you what is beautiful and what is not, there to lie with you under stars. Risen up with the northern lights a vision so ethereal and fantastic it might have danced in those heavenbound beams since the beginning of time is somehow to do with her. In the trees she lurks, in the sun's comfort-kiss and in the wind. These horses share her passion. Her words in the river run. Lordy, Lordy, what have I left behind?

Thus consumed, I found liberation with the Marlboro Man. Survivalist, backwoodsman, cowboy-hatted, lean and moustached, the strong and silent embodiment of masculinity on his Marlboro horse, Dave was the antidote to my sentimentality. I tried to imagine telling him about the relationship and sobered up quickly. You great English dude take this axe and cut me some deadfall from this path. See that horse there, he'll need shodding before he goes a step further. Take this shoe and don't get kicked. A great kicking up the backside was really what I got, for here it was all about survival. There was no time to be emotional for there was always something you had to be doing, and everything you did had to count. There was no time to think of the past, for faced with swamps and spooking horses the present became rather more important. Is there anywhere a more masculine rite of passage than herding horses through the Canadian Rockies pursued by the Marlboro Man? Chris was there of course, and she was not at all masculine, but she was doing masculine things all the same and she was the Marlboro Man's wife. She was not going to ruffle my hair.

"Free from those soft influences which are apt occassionally to occurrance," was how Milton's friend Teesdale had ineptly applauded the end of his engagement to Miss Dorcas Chichester. Milton escaped his soft influences by indulging in his own festival of machismo – crossing Canada with

Cheadle, La Ronde and the Assiniboine. That would have been sufficient to knock the softness out of anyone, and the Assiniboine's wife wasn't going to ruffle his hair. The Marlboro Man and eight horses were sufficient for me.

The path of the love-worn beaten across prairie and hill. Hurry west for salvation.

WHEN MEN AND
MOUNTAINS MEET

One night in the valley of the Athabasca River Milton sleep-talked. Cheadle records him often doing this, and woe betide anyone who woke Milton early after such a night, for those were his darkest mornings. "Crabbed and vicious," noted Cheadle. Tented out in wilderness, his frenzied mutterings must have sounded preposterous. O'Beirne, already unsettled, became unhinged:

> Milton woke up with a shout, and Mr O'B. cried out in terror, "Oh, dear! oh, dear! this is perfectly horrible – what has happened? *It's only me – O'B. – don't shoot, my lord!*" Every one then woke up, and there was a general commotion; but finding the alarm groundless, all returned to their blankets, except the unhappy cause of the disturbance

[O'Beirne], who remained sitting out the hours of darkness, too discomposed for sleep.

They were now in the central Rocky Mountain ranges near Jasper, borne down upon on all sides by mountains, and what effect would that have had on minds unused for a year to anything taller than trees? They all misjudged distances in the Rockies, a desert mile seems unlike a mountain mile, but big landscapes can draw out unforeseen psychologics and Milton could play out these in his sleep. Was he liberated or terrified in a landscape without fences, reassured or dominated in one without horizons? He'd have had to play these out at night for there was no time during the day. They had miles to make, rivers to cross.

The Athabasca was too deep and fast to ford so together they built a raft – all, that is, except for O'Beirne, who read his Paley's *Evidences of Christianity* and smoked a pipe. Confronted by Milton, he protested: "It's all very well for Cheadle with shoulders like the Durham ox to treat gigantic exertion of this kind so lightly, but I assure you it would very soon kill a man of my delicate constitution." When Cheadle pointed out that Milton was even slighter than him yet did his work without complaint, he riposted: "Ah yes. He is fired with emulation. I have been lost in admiration of his youthful ardour all the day." Milton's youthful ardour is well documented in *The North-West Passage by Land*. Perhaps too well documented. A succession of small heroic deeds mentioned in that book are strangely absent from Cheadle's diary:

Milton and the boy had volunteered to swim across with horses, in order to carry ropes to the other side with which to guide the raft – a somewhat hazardous adventure, as the river was broad, and the stream tremendously rapid. . . .

O'Beirne . . . suddenly plunged into a hole, where the water was nearly up to his arm-pits. He cried out wildly, 'I'm drowning! Save me! Save me!' then, losing his presence of mind, applied, in his confusion, the saying of his favourite poet, '*In medio tutissimus ibis*,' and struggled back to the shallow part. He was in imminent danger of being carried off, and Milton hastened to the rescue, and brought him out, clinging to his stirrup.

In Cheadle's diary O'Beirne is saved by a Hudson's Bay Company employee from Jasper House. Was Cheadle mistaken, or was Milton not quite the brave his readers were led to believe? They were led to believe an awful lot, and bravery was only part of it. At a wedding dance near Fort Garry the previous year, we are told that:

Milton, with a courage equal to the occasion, and, it is suspected, strongly attracted by the beauty of the bride – a delicate-featured, pensive-looking girl of sixteen or seventeen, with a light and graceful figure – boldly advanced, and led her out amid the applause of the company. He succeeded in interpreting the spirit of the music, if not with the energy, certainly with a greater dignity and infinitely less exertion than his compeers. His performance was highly appreciated by all – including Treemiss and Cheadle – who gazed with admiration, mingled with envy, at a success they were unequal to achieve.

He was not shy of a boast, and why should he be? Contained for so long in England, how he must have loved to let his spirit roam and know it would bring down no judgement. If his book is as embellished as my grandmother's stories then where does that leave the truth? And does that matter?

The Shuswap Indians who lived near Jasper House at that time were cut off from the main body of their tribe near Kamloops in British Columbia by four hundred miles of forest. Milton found them so impressive that he wrote what amounts almost to an academic study on them, a good portion of which made it into *The North-West Passage by Land*. He admired them for their peacefulness, their hardiness and their honesty, the same attributes for which he admired the Woods Cree. In particular he admired them for the way they wandered about in the snow in bare feet ("bear feet" as Milton put it), and for their tendency to camp in territory with the least shelter and to build the smallest campfires of "any other Indians I have ever seen although they have no enemies to fear." This ectopic band of staunch wildmen were only thirty-strong and heading for extinction on account of their perilous hunting methods: "They live by hunting the bighorns, mountain goats, and marmots; and numbers who go out every year never return. Like the chamois hunters of the Alps, some are found dashed to pieces at the foot of the almost inaccessible heights to which they follow their game; of others no trace is found." Such was Milton's respect for the locals (though he couldn't help himself referring to the first two Shuswap he met as "specimens").

They bought some whitefish from the Shuswap but nothing else and nothing from the traders at Jasper House, for although this was only July, food was never easy to find in the Rockies. O'Beirne at this point ran out entirely. His forty pounds of pemmican, which he had carried separately and which had been measured out to last the journey, he had devoured in under a month. Undaunted, he started tucking into Milton's and Cheadle's. "The prospect of starvation was discernible even now," they warned. Prescient of disasters looming they hired an extra guide at Jasper House, an elderly Iroquois Métis called Louis Caropontier who would help them to Tête Jaune Cache. Or rather Cheadle hired him, for Milton considered the Iroquois's fee of a horse exorbitant and was angry with Cheadle for going behind his back. The good doctor explained in his diary: "I should not have cared had I had one able-bodied man with me but to be left alone with Milton and O'Beirne to haul to Cariboo, would be too great an undertaking." Irrepressible pomposity! Who did he think he was, understating "MiLord's" considerable energies? Who was the boss here? The journey was undoubtedly Milton's project – it was his idea and probably paid for with his money – but he was only twenty-three and you sense from his diary that Cheadle felt a responsibility towards Milton that went beyond friendship. It was more a duty. If that meant he had to go behind

his back to help him through, then so be it. Egos will be
troubled, sparks will fly.

They had one river to cross, the Miette, before making the
Yellowhead Pass. Since it was too tempestuous to raft, they
elected to ford it mounted, to the horror of O'Beirne, who
entered the water flanked by Milton and the Assiniboine's
wife like some crusading prince:

> Clutching the mane with both hands, he did not attempt to
> guide his horse, but employed all his powers in sticking to
> the saddle, and exhorting his companions, "Steady, my
> lord, please, or I shall be swept off. *Do* speak to Mrs
> Assiniboine, my lord; she's leading us to destruction; what
> a reckless woman! *varium et mutabile semper femina!* Mrs
> Assiniboine! – *Mrs Assiniboine!* oh, dear! oh, dear! what an
> awful journey! I'm going! I'm going! Narrow escape that,
> my lord! very narrow escape, indeed, Doctor. We can't
> expect to be so lucky every time, you know."

In the woods some way north of Milton's route the sound
of our movement was thrown back to us and the noise of
horses and the noise of humans were one. It was a snorting,
stamping, deep-breathing factory of endeavour, the horses
stumbling over roots and fallen branches and flailing
through swamp and creek and swaying like drunken laundry
maids under their loads down the slopes and no one speaking save to urge them on. The smell of horse shit and the

creak of leather. This is no easy hack and no postcard pack train. Everything in its moment matters to the exclusion of all else and each moment when you are done with it is forgotten, and behind them all the only thing that matters is where you are tonight. This living in the present a blessed, prescripted relief.

We came across McLaren's Pass with the wide Snake Indian River valley laid out. The pass is close to treeline and the spruces on the pass grow to just a few feet, though in every other respect they are regular spruces, these high-altitude effigies. Mount Robson, the highest peak in the Canadian Rockies at 3,954 metres, is 25 miles directly to the southwest, though it is a great deal further on the ground and we would not be there for weeks. Lying almost back to back with the horses and harried by a young eagle we descended the steep pass westwards through late-blooming forget-me-nots and woolly fleabane and then we turned northwest up Blue Creek. This for all the world is like a Scottish trout stream with deep still pools and rocky overhangs and rapids; we should surely pull some trout from there. We camped under a vast limestone cliff known as Ancient Wall. The bedding in Ancient Wall is layered up and crazily folded and the whole face is weathered so that some beds are prominent and some cut away according to their hardness. With an eye on this and the colour consistent and particular to each layer you can trace a bed for several miles across the face. There is no growth on this monstrous appendage, this inanimate desert cliff, and above the productivity of the valley it looks otherworldly, a museum piece on loan from some other barren planet, vestiges of extinct life within. In the afternoon sunshine this cliff like all outsized formations appears to shift against the sky, it has cast off and lies untethered to the Earth.

Before leaving Jasper, Dave had sneaked a look at Cheadle's diary, and noting Milton's enthusiasm for rum slipped a bottle into our load. We might drink it, he said, or we might get to trade it. Pass it for marten furs, pemmican, knowledge of conditions ahead. We would meet no traders; this was simply Dave entering into the spirit. Hunkered down beside the fire every night on the trail he read extracts from the diary and weighed Milton's journey against ours, reckoned that with 180 pounds or more on each horse they packed a fair old load – we carried 150 pounds; reckoned too that with those loads and that number of packhorses they must have been planning on settling in that wilderness. I suggested they had probably planned for British Columbia's high society, which they would seek to impress on arrival in Victoria. Three-piece suits and morning dress cut to the standards of a viscount were hard to come by on that new frontier, so they must pack them all in though they be of dubious use on the trail.

Sartorial non-necessities aside, Dave thought their travelling must have been similar to ours, for the ground is unchanged and there are few ways of journeying with a horse in the mountains. Their trail was less travelled. We by law could not hunt with guns. They had O'Beirne, a thought Dave could not get straight in his head. But the forest now is as it was then, and the rivers and what spooks a horse and what troubles it have not altered. These horses are spooked by the bleached horn of a moose beside the way. They are troubled by bog and would sooner wade a large river than step into mud they do not have the measure of. The only way to get Comanche through mud was to get tough with him and often he would panic and skirt the mud into something worse, and then the packhorses would panic and cast off into the trees and unsettle their packs and that would be that. It was a struggle that Milton could appreciate:

> A day's journey on the road to Jasper House generally consists of floundering through bogs, varied by jumps and plunges over the timber which lies strewn, piled, and interlaced across the path and on every side. The horses stick fast in the mire, tumble crashing amongst the logs, or, driven to desperation, plunge amongst the thickly-growing trees at the side, where they are generally quickly brought up by the wedging of their packs in some narrow passage between contiguous trunks.

Beyond the Yellowhead Pass – so inconspicuous they only knew they'd crossed it when they noticed waters flowing Pacific-bound – the travelling got harder. The Fraser River, whose north bank they now followed, had flooded and they toiled through swamps and sodden deadfall and through waters up to the horses' bellies. There was nowhere to stop and no feed for the horses and they pressed on, this apocalyptic waterworld a challenge for any rider and Milton quite up to it. "Milton dragged on to the tail of his horse passing thro' thick bushes, but he held on and scrambled on again like a monkey without stopping," observed Cheadle. He was still going long after the others had quit and were leading theirs until he "at last confessed this beat hunting in Ireland, and dismounted, his saddle always slipping loose." O'Beirne, a fair-weather horseman, had succumbed long before. Cheadle found him scratched and muddied and his clerical coat "split asunder" from the neck like some vagrant highwayman brought to earth. "Very nearly killed, Doctor, this time. I thought it was all over. *Semel est calcanda via lethi*, you know. My horse fell and rolled on to me, tearing my coat, as you see. I've had a most providential escape."

This rough country drew out in Milton his most implacable demons. Cheadle records in several thousand words three days of Miltonian unrest. It is a chronicle of emotional anarchy. There is no suggestion from the Doctor of an epileptic trigger but a character shaped by severe epilepsy is often angry, and the bigger the ego the more angry it might be. Milton raged at the guides for making camp too late. He raged at Cheadle for breaking camp too early. He raged at the horses for their stubbornness. A malcontent crying in the wilderness, these restless spirits will out.

> Milton in a great passion ... began abusing me, & the guide for going on & we had a grand quarrel. It had been brewing for several days, & its first origin was that Milton had

neither the patience, activity or constant attention necessary to drive horses in the woods. I got on famously & had mine always close at the heels of the guide, whilst he was always in difficulties & calling out for the rest to stop. I bullied him tremendously about this & recommended him not to drive any more, taking two myself, he having left his to his fate in a great temper.... We had both completely lost temper that I would not stop to quarrel & walked off.... We went to bed with the matter unadjusted, Milton giving orders that we should not start early because he wished to write his journal, & dry some "bois gris"! (Cheadle's diary)

"*Bois gris*" was the bark of the red osier dogwood which like bearberry or "kinnikinnik" makes a decent tobacco. A good smoke was what Milton needed, and something stronger if Cheadle kept up his sanctimoniousness. He may have been a fine doctor but he was no therapist. On the other hand, an angry and upset Milton was hard to accommodate.

Milton's epilepsy is not even hinted at in *The North-West Passage by Land*. It was something people kept quiet about and it would not have made him appear heroic. It is more interesting that Cheadle barely mentions it in his diary. True to his fastidious character, the Doctor kept detailed notes throughout the journey on all things medical – Indians with suspected smallpox, Milton's frostbite, his own Achilles strain, tetanus in a dog – but he only occasionally mentions the main thing for which he was there at all. Sometimes he observes Milton as "seedy" or suffering "symptoms" – strange feelings physical or emotional such

as paranoia, depersonalization, hallucinations and especially headaches that often precede or follow a fit. But these
seem to have disappeared after a good sniff of rum or a
smoke. The only occasions on which he would record an
"attack" were in Victoria, British Columbia, shortly before
they return to England. For the preceding year and a half
Milton had been completely free of fits. There could hardly
be a stronger indication of how good for him were the challenge and the openness of Canada and how bad the social
pressures of his life in England.

On this occasion he was brought from his underworld by
a shared misfortune that was sufficiently levelling for them
both to laugh at. After passing the "immeasurably supreme"
Mount Robson, two of their packhorses, Bucephalus and
Gisquakarn, or "The Fool" as they called him, fell into the
Fraser. A mile downstream they found them standing
forlorn in some shallows in the middle of the river. They
tried calling them to the bank, made tempting offers of
pasture and oats. Bucephalus, convinced, made for shore.
The Fool cast off into the current with his load and was
never seen again. This was unfortunate. The horse's pack
held their most valuable belongings – though they were
hardly crucial to their survival. Cheadle lost his sextant,
revolver, powder and caps, cash box, watch, ring, breastpin,
papers, letters, tea, all his tobacco and his botanical collection. Milton lost his best suit, great coat, moccasins, silk
handkerchiefs, shirts, socks, letters of introduction, credit
papers, chequebook, passport and all his tobacco. I suddenly felt underequipped. What was I doing crossing the

Prairie monuments: winter and summer on
the Carlton Trail, Saskatchewan

La Belle Prairie, Saskatchewan, 136 years after
Milton and Cheadle spent the winter

Supposed site of Fort Milton, Devil's (Morin) Lake, La Belle Prairie

Rose and Bronco (seated), Louis La Ronde's great-great-grandchildren, with Earlin, Rose's son (right)

With Sam Joseph (Keenamontiayoo) and two of his grandchildren, at the Big River Reserve

Sam and grandchild outside his cabin

Sam with his wife, his son
Barry, and grandchildren

The hunter: George
Joseph, Sam's brother

George Joseph and a cousin smoking moose meat in his garden

The far country: into the heart of the Rockies

They stumbled over rocks and they played up in water but those horses went just about anywhere we asked them to go.

With Chris and Dave outside the cabin at
Miette Lake, Rocky Mountains

Summer to winter in a night. Heading southwest
towards the Miette Pass

Coming out of the mountains. Me on Comanche, with
stubborn old Hector in tow

Rockies without a suit? Milton had lost only his best suit, so presumably he had several others with him, but what would he do in British Columbia without silk handkerchiefs? O'Beirne lost his letters of introduction, his kettle, and a pair of spectacles. Thankfully for everyone in the party he did not lose his *Evidences of Christianity*, but since his remaining pair of spectacles had only one lens, reading it would now pose him a considerable challenge. If Milton hoped it might keep him quiet he was disappointed.

ENCHANTED FOREST

People talk about the healing powers of horses. Just ride them, they say, and you'll understand. But it takes time before you notice anything and it's when you've stopped thinking about it that it has started to work. It is all about passion. Some talk about the intelligence of horses, but is it intelligence when they shy at a corpse or try to pass Houdini-like between gaps too small for their packs? Distressed at the temporary absence of a fellow horse, why can they not rationalize that he will return as he has always done? Not much of what Comanche and the others did could you put down to intelligence, but everything they did you could put down to passion.

It is the way a horse responds to the world that gets to you, living as he does moment by moment. If all his heart is invested in where his hoof goes next or how he can reach that five-star tuft of grass lurking forestwards, then it pretty soon becomes the only important thing to you too. He responds to what he gets. He will bow his head to the rain, he will step ballet-wise downhill. When he stumbles you stumble, you fall with him. The mountain trail is rough and through the horse you feel every inch of it and through the horse you lose yourself. Or rather you lose your worrying, which mixes poorly with all that passion, and unencumbered you are yourself again. I started to forget about the girl. Except that you don't even get to think that, for you are on a perilous cliff-path and the horse is getting agitated by a horsefly and there seems too little room on that path for a horse to get agitated. That is how horses heal.

One afternoon on the Snake Indian River we turned them out into meadows that were boggy and thin on grass. They needed a good feed, so when we found some better meadows upstream of the camp we went to harry them out of the marshland and into the good pasture for a full night of feasting. They took some finding among the willow and soapberry and they were scattered about, each feeding on his own meagre patch of rough growth. Comanche characteristically was in the middle of a bog. Unclipping his hobbles and tying his halter into reins I jumped on saddleless and a little precarious and we were off, pushing the packhorses ahead through the willow-scrub and the horses getting excited and jumpy and we shouting at them to settle. Clinging on through the grasping undergrowth we hazed them out through the marshland in a haphazard and spirited stampede, a company of equine delinquents. You can feel every tensing in your horse's back, you shape the ground through him, but who knows what else a horse passes to his bareback rider that his bareback rider doesn't figure. I felt changed every time I rode like that, a little freer, a little more at peace. You're pretty sure you'll change back again but do it often enough and it might stick.

We still had sunshine. In the evenings we had high-definition postcard worlds painted by numbers, each tree, cloud or rockface assigned a colour particular to it and out standing against its background, each thing cast from a different mould. We had daisy fleabane, monkshood, buttercup, goldenrod, potentilla, sagebrush, juniper, silverberry and white clover, Labrador tea which you can drink and kinnikinnik to smoke. At night we had cold, and we had the sound of water. Going to sleep beside rivers I always thought I heard the words. Freed from the minds that conjured them up they might have been spoken in anger but they fell over the rocks in peace, a universal conversation. Through the rivers run all the words of the dead. I could hear whomever I chose to hear: my grandmother in excitement over grizzlies, my father in approval of me in this place, Milton concerned how I might portray him in this book. Nothing this river said could harm me, all it threw out was poetry. We had other workings of that wilderness that you cannot imagine until you are in it.

In the middle of September Dave left us to scout ahead and to clear some trails that we would use later on. He was gone for days, a loner loning, a doer doing. He left me with

Chris on the Snake Indian River and that was an adventure in itself. She might have been Dave for all her skill with the horses and her knowledge of the country and travelling through it horsewise, but not for all the blonde hair and not for the noise. It was like a travelling circus now. Laughter and Indian war-whoops from within the muted woods. A little longer to break camp in the mornings and a little more chaos. Stories around the campfire of men who have hired her to take them into the mountains to hunt and their hopeless advances under starlight, and her parrying. I said it was very trusting of Dave to leave her with me, especially given the reputation of my ancestor, and she wondered if I meant trusting of me or trusting of her. I said I was sure he trusted her, but how could he be so sure of me? Ah, she smiled, he knows I could deal with you with one arm tied. You, an Englishman in a Canadian forest, without me are lost. It was an immutable and unpalatable truth to which Milton would never have submitted so easily.

They amused themselves by naming mountains: "Milton chose a fine hill to the left as his mountain, & I a still higher to the right. His cone-like & terraced, mine a long range of very rugged rocks, very high & snow-clad with green slopes, & bright pines half way up. Very fine indeed." (Cheadle's diary). The Iroquois guide assured them that from then on those mountains would be known as "Le Montagne de Milord" and "Le Montagne de Docteur," though they opted

for Mount Fitzwilliam and Mount Bingley, after Cheadle's
home town in Yorkshire. You can see these mountains when
you come through the Yellowhead Pass. They also named
nearby Rockingham Creek and there are Rockingham Falls
and Mount Rockingham, and Bucephalus Peak, named by a
surveyor after the explorers' accident-prone horse, which
was immortalized in *The North-West Passage by Land*.

Between Tête Jaune Cache and Kamloops they marked
down for each other Mount Milton and Mount Cheadle,
and Mount St. Anne and Little Hell's Gate Rapids on the
North Thompson, and Milton named the Wentworth River
after his home, the Malton Range after another of his family's
estates, the Shillelagh River after the village at Coollattin,
Albreda Lake after his aunt, the Elsecar River after his father's
coal mine and the Murchison Rapids after the president of
the Royal Geographical Society. Some of these names stuck
and some didn't. How are such things named? When surveyors came to the Yellowhead area in the 1950s they might ask
four Indians the name of a mountain and they'd get four
different names, depending on which side of the mountain
the Indian lived. These perks of an Empire-builder. Mount
Fitzwilliam has a perfect diamond top and it is the shape a
child would draw a mountain. It is an aristocratic mountain. Milton must have had an eye for these things, for Mount
Milton is similar. Mount Bingley, today known as Bingley
Peak, is expansive and bulldog-faced but it is nearly four
hundred metres lower than Mount Fitzwilliam, and more
than a hundred metres lower than a peak later named Mount
O'Beirne. Milton would have enjoyed that.

At Tête Jaune Cache where the Fraser turns northwest they could have followed the river all the way to what is now Prince George and the Cariboo, like the majority of the Overlanders the year before, who had headed off on rafts beset by morale-boosting cries from the Indians of "Poor White Man No More!" Instead they took the advice of the local Shuswap and went south towards the North Thompson River. The Indians, however, were hardly better informed, one old lady (later cursed by Cheadle as a "wretched old imposter") assuring Milton he would make it to Kamloops in eight days. Milton, the accumulator of mechanical fancies, acquired two stone smoking-pipes from these dispensers of misinformation, though he had nothing to smoke in them, and some large cubes of iron pyrites for lighting his fires. Into the unknown went the party, and under a great illusion.

Two days later they were fortunate still to be alive. To get to the Upper Thompson valley they had to cross a tributary of the Columbia River called the Canoe and their crossing of this river features in a drawing and over five pages of text in *The North-West Passage by Land*, so well did it illustrate what they were up against. They drove the horses across and cut down trees for a raft, which with their one small axe took them half the day. On this hopeful contrivance, no doubt engineered by Milton, they set off with their provisions into the current:

We were helplessly borne straight to what seemed certain destruction, a large pine-tree, through the lower branches of which the water rushed like the stream from a mill-wheel. "A terre – a terre avec la line!" shouted The Assiniboine, as we neared the bank for an instant, and making a desperate leap into the water caught the bushes, scrambled up the side, and whipped his rope round a tree. Cheadle jumped at the same moment with the other rope, and did likewise; but the cords, rotten from repeated wettings, snapped like threads, the raft was sucked under the tree, and disappeared beneath the water. Milton and the woman were brushed off like flies by the branches, but Mr O'B., in some incomprehensible manner, managed to stick to the raft, and reappeared above water further down, sitting silent and motionless, sailing along to swift destruction with seeming resignation.

O'Beirne was saved by the Assiniboine. Milton was saved by Cheadle, as illustrated in my favourite passage in *The North-West Passage by Land*:

Cheadle, with a confused notion that everybody was drowned but himself, heard a cry proceeding from the tree, and looking in that direction, observed Milton clinging to the branches, his body sucked under the trunk, and his head disappearing under water and rising again with the varying rush of the current. The woman was in similar position, but further out and on the lower side. Both were in imminent danger of being swept off every moment, and Cheadle, shouting to them for God's sake to hold on, clambered along the tree and laid hold of Milton, who was nearest. He cried out to help the woman first, but Cheadle, seeing the woman was more difficult to reach, and Milton in the greater danger, helped him out at once.

Therein lies everything expected of a nineteenth-century explorer: a dramatic encounter with something wild, a near-death experience, an heroic gesture towards a fellow traveller (preferably female) and the unblinking loyalty of a friend. *He cried out to help the woman first* sounds suspiciously like a piece of Miltonesque embroidery, but it is confirmed in Cheadle's diary, in which he describes his partner as "noble," Milton's actual words apparently being: "Never mind me, help the woman." A hero after all and how could I have doubted?

O'Beirne, needless to say, was beside himself. "I've had a terrible shock today – a terrible shock! *Mihi frigidus horror membra quatit.* I'm trembling with the recollection of it now. Ah! Doctor, Doctor, you don't know what I suffered. *Heu me miserum! iterum iterumque, strepitum fluminum audio!*" The only thing that really bothered Milton was the loss of their cooking equipment, which meant they had to cook their pemmican and flour in a kettle. He and Cheadle missed their tobacco, but most of all they missed their tea.

They reached the North Thompson and, still harbouring dreams of cutting directly to the goldfields of Cariboo, dispatched the Assiniboine in reconnaissance northwestwards along that river. He returned soon afterwards declaring the forest impenetrable and progress impossible, at least with one little axe, a pack of worn-down horses – and O'Beirne. "Sulkily," and on Milton's twenty-fourth birthday, July 27, they set their minds again to the southern route to Kamloops. They were running short of food, but they had found a trail left by the Overlanders the year before and an inscription marking where their guide André Cardinal had left them. Milton expected to reach Kamloops in a few days. It was an ill-placed expectation.

One evening east of the Snake Indian Pass with the horses staked out and a black-backed woodpecker in camp working pieces of bark from a dying spruce, Chris and I walked out in search of elk lurking predator-wise in the forest. At the height of the rut an elk is mercurial, prone to unlikely behaviour, though its cry is like a strangled train whistle and hardly imperative. Blinded by testosterone, elk have been known to mount tethered horses; you can tell such a horse by the antler scars along its flanks. Chris has trailed many elk and she says their sense of hearing, smell and sight are better than in any other deer. They are certainly better than ours, for that evening we hardly got near them.

If you want to see wild animals on the trail a pack of horses is the last thing you need and this lot was like a marauding tribe, a class of schoolchildren on a seaside outing. There was feeding on the sly, shunting for position, bottom-biting and attempted short cuts. No wild animal will wait around to seek the cause of such infantile commotion. But the animals were out there and they had left tracks and scats and we must construct their world from such clues. Up the Snake Indian River we followed moose and elk, and a bear sow and cub. Pray that we do not fall upon her even with horses, said Chris, who is unaccustomed to being among bears unarmed.

We rode up out of the forest and crossed the Snake Indian Pass in the sunshine, there to the northeast a monstrous wall of sheet limestone, upended beds folded and eroded on the plane to a sculptural improbability. Foundering in the marsh in the valley on the other side Comanche began to lose heart and had to be led. He did his best to tread around the problems by going off track where he encountered just the hazards he sought to avoid. He was not brave, this horse, he was not clever and his main concern was to fill his stomach, but at least he was not crazy and he had not yet tried to buck me off. He was tough like all these outback horses. I loved his moods and I loved to ride him through his troubles. He never seemed sure that he would overcome them but he always did. He stumbled but he never fell. It takes some time to trust a horse and for him to trust you and then you imagine he will carry you anywhere.

Into Twintree Lake, which boomerangs south to north-west five miles tip to tip and is hedged all the way by the spruce forest, flows Twintree Creek and out again, and where the water leaves the lake I hooked a rainbow trout which we fried for supper. A fish prepared with great ceremony as if for a religious feast-day and as fresh a fish as I am likely to taste. Bedded down in those hills afterwards I drifted off to the horse-bells and the sound of the creek and I felt a deep happiness, and all that I had left behind felt a long way behind.

The next morning I could still hear the bells but they were ringing on ghosts of horses. The horses sounded close to camp but after searching all morning through the trees we had none to speak of, though still they rang about us. They had learnt to climb and were taunting us from the treetops. They had hobble-hopped to the other side of the lake and their bells were coming to us over miles of water. They had been spirited off in the night to a world not of their choosing and they would haunt these woods forevermore. We found them eventually hardly half a mile from camp but up the northeast side of the valley. From such a height sounds carry irregularly to those on the ground. Chris remembers losing her horses on a hunting trip and finding them after a whole day's searching less than a mile from camp, bunched together and immobile among the trees, bells hanging unsounded from their necks. Possessed by the horse-spirit of stillness what those horses knew she could not guess at.

They were used to seeing O'Beirne rooted and book in hand when hard work beckoned, so when crossing to the west bank of the Thompson they observed him skipping goat-like across the logs, they thought his Christian text had finally got the better of him and that it was a changed man who approached them. Instead it was self-preservation that he had in mind for he was being chased by the Assiniboine. Finding O'Beirne sitting idle, he had "advanced towards him with so menacing an air that he fled across the bridge with great celerity, and took his share of work without complaint. Mr O'B. firmly believed that The Assiniboine intended to murder him on the first convenient opportunity, and viewed any offensive demonstration on his part with unqualified terror."

If O'Beirne had known what they were in for next, he might have chosen rough treatment at the hands of the Assiniboine. About twenty miles further on, the Overlanders' trail south finished in sawdust and fallen trees. Here, evidently, they had given up the idea of cutting a way through the forest, slaughtered their remaining cattle and taken to the river. Given their recent experiences with rafts, this was not an attractive option for Milton's party. The Upper Thompson was turbulent, rocky and long. Instead they would have to make their own trail through the untravelled forest with their undersized axe and wretched horses. They had food for a few more days. They reckoned Kamloops was one hundred and thirty miles away and it was no longer looking like a stroll. Cheadle considered these tidings "evil" but noted that Milton was "indifferent." Perhaps things were still too tame for "MiLord." Without exceptional circumstances there can be no heroes. O'Beirne, back to his melodramatic self, predicted a miserable end for them all. They had plenty to reflect on: "We held grave council over our campfire, trying to increase philosophy by smoking kinnikinnick."

They also had plenty to squabble over. The chances of them agreeing in a crisis were slim since such occasions appeared

to heighten both Cheadle's intolerance and Milton's insou-
ciance. The deeper the fix, the more relaxed Milton
became, and the more outraged Cheadle. Milton had developed into a champion Cheadle-baiter, and he was safe in
this, for despite his friend's seniority in age and his
resourcefulness and medical expertise on which he himself
depended, this was still Milton's show. It was enough to
make a young viscount reckless. It was enough to turn a
good doctor sulphurous:

> Milton will delay to have moccasins made, although I
> offered to lend him a pair to enable us to go forward to some
> feeding for the horses. Much squabbling between us during
> last few days, & I have now completely resigned all share in
> management or rather such mismanagement. I myself thor-
> oughly sick of such childish work. (Cheadle's diary).

Given the idiosyncracies of its members, it is a wonder this
unlikely group stayed united.

The forest through which they stumbled was fit for a
world of colossi but hardly for men of this world; it was a
forest of grotesques born out of some preposterous cata-
clysm. "No one who has not seen a primeval forest, where
trees of gigantic size have grown and fallen undisturbed for
ages, can form any idea of the collection of timber, or the
impenetrable character of such a region," wrote Milton.
There were pines and cedars three hundred feet high with
gargantuan trunks. Prostrate, such trees laid out like enor-
mous spilt matches form fortress walls against the traveller.

Through this fantasy land they drove their listless horses and through swamps shoulder-high with thorned devil's club. Little wonder that the horses were reluctant to move forward "except under the stimulus of repeated blows." The party managed just three miles a day, sometimes barely one. Worn through with the physical effort and consumed by the melancholy of this forest and by its monstrosity, these jaunty adventure-men began to doubt seriously for the first time in a year. "The work was vexatious and wearisome in the extreme, and we found our stock of philosophy quite unequal to the occasion." So serious was their fix that O'Beirne gave up on his Paley's *Evidences of Christianity*, which he had read every day since leaving Edmonton, even declaring some of its propositions shaky. In earthquakes are foundations tested.

We moved through dead fallen trees disarranged and cushioned on the feather moss and resting in the limbs of willows in the filtered sunlight like soldiers in the arms of nurses. Sentried by the unfallen dead stood upright and branchless like telegraph poles we passed wild rose and juniper, clusters of mushrooms and occasional poplars misplaced among the spruce and fir, the living nourished by the dead. We saw mushrooms in the branches of trees. Sprung heavenward from the earth, how had those fungi risen? The unaccountable workings of a fairytale forest. It is something like Milton's forest, though our path was mostly cut. It was a rough path and steep and sometimes treacherous in the rock slides, and we often had to stop to see to the packs. During such stops Comanche set to feeding. He was renamed "Comunchie." Northwest of Twintree Lake, Chris's horse Spook stepped into a deep bog and floundered and pitched her off and lay still on his back too terror-stricken to climb out. There he remained for some minutes weathering fearsome profanities from Chris, and we had virtually to drag him from it. These things kept us watchful. Still we were not troubled by a lack of food nor hounded by any self-appointed sergeant-major, though I knew the pace would step up when Dave returned. We had nothing to smoke and did not fancy kinnikinnik. My trousers were stiff with mud and I was dirty and sore and a sight for the great-aunts. It was getting cold at nights. Still, I was a whole lot better in the mornings than Milton.

We forded the Smoky River and we followed upstream the wide gravel floodplain and scattered across it lay pieces of driftwood from the spring floods weathered into cadaverous forms. Bleached and petrified they resembled skeleton, skull and horn, and the riverplain the aftermath of an immense slaughter. We ranged through this dreamscape and found pasture in the trees a few miles up and here we camped, sleeping out and watching shooting stars through the canopy as the horses belled about and the river ran on. These things would wake you up every hour or so and each time it strikes you how the stars have shifted, how the moon lights differently, how there are clouds where none were. Change haunts these nights and days. The sun always rises and the stars turn but there is plenty of room for chaos.

We carried on south the next day and we rode up once again into the heather and stunted conifers of the upper subalpine and in the late afternoon we came out into a valley at the head of which stands Mount Robson, which straddles the border between British Columbia and Alberta. Further up the valley there is an old warden's cabin and a logbook in which park rangers have noted down the affairs of this place. The first entry, dated 1979, is a lament for a girl called Karen, who was killed by a black bear in the forest nearby. She had been working in the mountains as a naturalist and the warden who wrote this knew her and had seen her often on the trail. He was distraught for he had been only minutes behind her that day and if only he had not stopped to put on his lace-up boots. We had seen a black bear climbing down a rock slide the previous day and there are many diggings about. Chris says they are more dangerous than grizzlies for they will try to eat you if you play dead. If they attack you they are trying to kill you but if you fight back hard enough they will probably retreat. Did Karen play dead? The warden would mull it over in his mind and up there in that cabin he would have had too much time to think about it.

There were moose tracks near our camp and Chris practised her cow calls. We awaited a rampant herd of bulls but it never came. I set to tickling bull trout in the stream. They were having none of it. You need to bring your hand under them without them seeing you, but it was too bright and they were skittish fish. Chris was quite impressed; she said she had never seen it done. She still hadn't seen it done when I lost my balance and slipped into the water. Any half-dead or sleeping fish not yet startled now got the message. "The Englishman's pièce de résistance," remarked Chris.

It was hard to impress Chris, for there was not much about horses and the backcountry that she did not know. She liked to tease me about my Englishness. From the great-great-grandson of a lord she expected airs and graces, sharp tweeds and breeches, a manservant perhaps. Boxes of tea and cocktails at sundown. Since I was Milton's descendant she expected late starts and a temper. When would I reveal this lordliness? In what state for a lord are those trousers, and in what state that hair? She teased me about my accent. I assured Chris that I was four generations from being a lord, that while Milton may have worn sharp breeches at home, when in Canada he had adopted Indian dress, and that I normally didn't bother brushing my hair in London let alone in the Rocky Mountains and my friends usually suffered it if not my mother. Milton's hair by the time he reached British Columbia was past his shoulders and he wore a red bandana, though he was an atypical lord. A long-haired, late-rising lord, said Chris. And you only a long-haired Englishman.

It was peaceful at Mount Robson until the weather came in. This valley has inspired many people. "Here on the dust of countless ages past, I stand, this moment is my life," is carved outside the warden's cabin. What that dedicant found I sought, and if I ever found it it was in that valley. When past, present and future are one. We laid up and rested the horses. I wrote up my journal and threw stones at marmots, which look like seals from a distance the way they lie there sentinelling on rocks. Chris told me about a marmot on Snowbird Pass, where the Smoky River rises to the east of Robson, that liked to lick walkers' trousers. She has met people who have had their trousers licked by this deviant. The insane workings of this highland wilderness.

Milton's party ran out of food on August 8, their last meal a "rubbaboo" of pemmican boiled in water with a handful of flour. They calculated they had three or four days to Kamloops, which worried them, but not as much as it would have done had they known the truth about the rest of the journey, which would be measured in weeks rather than days. Milton because of his epilepsy which could flare up under extreme stress could not starve for long, so if they failed to kill any game they would have to shoot a horse. They took a day's rest to hunt but all they bagged was a marten. At dawn the next day the Assiniboine dispatched Blackie, the thinnest and most wretched of their horses, with "a ball behind the ear," and

> in a few minutes steaks were roasting at the fire, and all hands were at work cutting up the meat into thin flakes for jerking. All day long we feasted to repletion on the portions we could not carry with us, whilst the rest was drying over a large fire; for although doubts had been expressed

beforehand as to whether it would prove palatable, and
Milton declared it tasted of the stable, none showed any
deficiency of appetite.

They did not look for portents but what they found near
their camp the day they shot the horse seemed so apposite
that many readers of *The North-West Passage by Land*
accused them of making it up. There at the foot of a pine
tree sat an upright human corpse without its head. The legs
were crossed and the arms clasped over the knees, brown
skin stretched like parchment over the bones. Before it lay a
heap of ashes, around about a small axe, a kettle, a fishing
line and hooks, a knife, shot, fire-lighting tools. Close by
they found the bones of a horse cut into small pieces from
which this Indian had sucked every trace of meat before
dying of starvation in front of his fire. They could not find
his head, but given the position of the cervical vertebrae it
had not apparently been removed in violence. The decapi-
tation may have been a mystery but the cause of his death
was not, and its significance was not lost on any of them.

Our spirits, already sufficiently low from physical weakness
and the uncertainty of our position, were greatly depressed
by this somewhat ominous discovery. The similarity
between the attempt of the Indian to penetrate through the
pathless forest – his starvation, his killing of his horse for
food – and our own condition was striking. His story had
been exhibited before our eyes with unmistakable clearness
by the spectacle we had just left: increasing weakness;

hopeless starvation; the effort to sustain the waning life by sucking the fragments of bones; the death from want at last. We also had arrived at such extremity that we should be compelled to kill a horse. The Indian had started with one advantage over us; he was in his own country – we were wanderers in a strange land. We were in the last act of the play. Would the final scene be the same?

This grim melodrama was played out in newspapers and literary circles after the book was published and to Milton's chagrin it became a more enduring symbol of their journey than all his worthy political ambitions for the free settlement of Western Canada. He shouldn't have worried, for it helped draw people's attention to the place and set in motion the very changes he advocated. Some critics used the story of the headless Indian to try to discredit the entire book, declaring it a stunt to pull in an audience. Indignant, Milton published a postscript to a later edition with an account from Sandford Fleming's surveying party, which travelled up the North Thompson in 1872. One of the party found the skeleton with its attendant apparatus scattered by the fallen pine tree. He found the missing skull fifty yards away. He buried the skeleton, placed the skull on top of the grave and left the epitaph: "Here lie the remains of the headless Indian discovered by Lord Milton and Dr. Cheadle, 1863." The skull was removed a few months later by Dr. Moran, another of Sandford's men, who took it to the offices of the Canadian Pacific Railway Survey in Ottawa, where it was accidentally cremated in 1874 when the building burnt down.

None of this explains how the Indian lost his head. James White in the *Canadian Alpine Journal* suggested that Cheadle himself had removed and hidden it. Fleming's surveyors fingered the Assiniboine, claiming he had killed, decapitated, eaten and redressed the man before alerting the others. Milton blamed a wild animal. The most remarkable thing is that it took nine years for someone else to find it. "This . . . testifies more forcibly than words can do to the intense solitude, and to the absence of human or animal life of any kind, which characterise the dense and lonely forests of the North Thompson," wrote Milton. "No human being, and, seemingly, no hungry or destructive carnivor of any kind, had passed that way in the long interval since we turned our faces away from the ominous scene, on the 8th of August, 1863."

DELIVERANCE

The night the weather turned we were still sleeping out under the stars, but it was the last time, for that was when the summer ended and we never did see autumn. By dawn the cloud was down and the wind was coming up the valley off Mount Robson and we were taking the rain hard in the face and the horses were not happy. We turned east off the Smoky River and over the long Moose Pass which was devoid of trees and you'd be pushed to find a more exposed piece of ground. In that cold, driven rain huddled up on a horse it was as miserable a time as any we spent on the trail. Then it started to snow. Within an hour the snow was an inch deep and it settled everywhere and it covered the trail. Chris had never been down the Moose River and she was guessing the way. She did pretty well in the whiteout. I would still be there. There were big trees across the trail and we had to get tough with the horses to get them across. They hated us and they hated this day. Comanche walked like a drunk, with his head turned away from the wind. Spook tumbled in a bog again and Chris was having a bad time of it. We had followed the diggings of a grizzly bear for miles across the pass and into the Moose Valley and the final straw, she said, would be to meet that bear out here without a gun.

It was like that for days. This was a different kind of travelling and in a way I was glad, for we had had it easy with all the sunshine and if I wasn't going to starve or fall out with my guide then I might as well have some other way of suffering. Milton suffered plenty up here but he didn't get snow. These valleys under snow are desolate and you are fortressed in by snow-laden mountains. You remember the great stillness and the mist off the rivers over the moon, but when you are in it all you want to do is get through.

On any other August 12, Milton might have been shooting grouse on some Scottish moor, indulged in roast game and fine wine and the company of women. On August 12, 1863, he got by on a few strips of horse meat, though he did bag a porcupine.

Several days south from the site of the headless Indian the North Thompson channels into rapids, and they passed beside these and came up against a high cliff that they had to scale. Such endeavour with worn-out horses led to another *North-West Passage* drama as unlikely as the rest. They led their horses over, all except O'Beirne, who appeared at the top without Bucephalus. "He's gone, killed, tumbled over a precipice," he panted. "*Facilis descensus*, you see. He slipped and fell over – ἔπειτα πέδονδε κυλίνδετο ΙΠΠΟΣ αναίδιησ, you know, and I have not seen him since. It's not the slightest use going back, I assure you, to look for him, for he's *comminuted*, smashed to atoms, dashed to a thousand pieces! It's a dreadful thing, isn't it?" They went back. The drop was a hundred and thirty feet from the ledge over a precipice to the river. Imagining Bucephalus *comminuted*, Cheadle climbed down to look.

On a little flat space below he saw Bucephalus, astride of a large tree, lengthwise. The tree was propped up by others horizontally at such a height that the animal's legs hung down on each side without touching the ground. The two then descended, expecting to find him mortally injured, but, to their astonishment, he appeared quite comfortable in his novel position.

They led him back to the path unharmed and mused on the charmed lives of horses.

They had a few charges of shot and some dried horse meat and little energy. They had no idea how far they were from Kamloops and often they were not sure whether it was the North Thompson they were following or some other river of no return. For five weeks they had seen no other human being. The Assiniboine became grumpy, wondering why

Milton and Cheadle if they were as aristocratic as they claimed had not recruited a bigger party and "done the thing in style." O'Beirne declared that his faith had been sapped to its foundations and that he was rapidly becoming insane, a descent Milton suggested the old pedagogue had begun years before. Even Cheadle took to reminiscing:

I think of home & its comforts, & the eatables & drinkables till we are quite wild with appetite for them. And then we have no tobacco! What would I give for 1lb shag & a yard of clay, a quart of beer! But I cannot stand this, I must change my thoughts, & resort to gnawing the shoulder blade of a horse." (Cheadle's diary).

Milton, as was his habit when stressed, took to arguing. "Very irritating and provoking," concluded Cheadle, and worse:

I have suffered horribly from anxiety the last few weeks on Milton's account. Apathetic, holding back, utterly reckless of the value of time, not appreciating the awkwardness of our position, I having no fear for myself but for him on account of his being unable to walk or endure prolonged fatigue in case of emergency. (Cheadle's diary).

One morning, Milton picked an argument with the Assiniboine's son over some inconsequence which ended with the thirteen-year-old pulling out his gun and pointing it at Milton's head. There are few more effective ways to end a debate. Milton later picked an argument with the Assiniboine himself, after which the guide threatened to desert. Cheadle reckoned it would take little more provocation before he did. In anger were this epileptic's passions spent, trivialities rendered critical by rage.

On Sunday, August 16, they shot another skeletal horse. It might have tasted of the stable but they feasted as if it had been prepared for the table at Wentworth.

Coming south in a snowstorm at the end of September and treading the riverbank for the best ground, we had eyes for a path heading east up the pass on the other side when the bank gave and took three horses with it into the river, Spook among them. Chris screamed as she was shunted into the stream. It was not deep and we got the horses out, but she was wet to the skin and up to her knees in the Moose River in a whiteout. Could things get any worse for her? She swore savagely, and then she laughed. She always suffered because she always went first and she never complained. She knocked the socks off Mrs. Assiniboine and she knocked them off the Assiniboine himself. She teased me about the English thing and the lord-chasing but I never minded. She kept feeding me with chocolate and looking out for me, but never too much. She let me do my bit.

The path we eventually chose on the east of the Moose River was harder than anything we'd done. No one had been through that way since a wildfire in the spring, and this fire had killed every tree for miles. The trunks stood tarred and traumatized on the smoking earth. There was deadfall everywhere and pushing the horses over it or cutting it out or skirting it we did barely half a mile in two hours. The horses held back at everything this hell-forest presented and they would flee off track if they could. They were spooked just by being there. They needed pushing and pulling to get them over the logs and they needed shouting at and sometimes they needed more. At a large fallen pine, Chris took a stick to stubborn old Hector's backside while I tugged on his leading-rope, for he would have stood at that tree until he starved. Indignant, Hector reared up and fell back on his haunches, which was distressing for him but not as distressing as it was for Coal, to whose tail Hector had been tied to keep him on the pace. Coal was stuck the other side of the tree and he was fast losing his tail. There was pandemonium and the sound of troubled horses. Chris shouted that Hector was strangling himself and she didn't have her knife. I fumbled out my penknife and slashed at the rope, which was quivering like taut elastic under the strain, and when it gave Hector jerked backwards and for a few seconds looked as if he'd go right over with the weight of his pack. He flailed wildly in the air with his front legs and then he came back down on all fours, snorting and shaking with the effort and the fear of it all. Coal looked affronted but at least he still had most of his tail. In *The North-West Passage by Land* there is a picture that shows Milton and Cheadle meting out similar punishment to a horse, beating and pulling it uphill near Jasper House. This was one of the incidents the Royal

Geographical Society banned Milton from mentioning in his lecture, and doubtless I have also now ruined my chances with that incorruptible institution.

Halfway up to Colonel Pass we found fresh-cut blazes on some of the trees. Whoever had left them had also cut a way through the deadfall with a chainsaw, and they had passed only a few hours before because the woodchips were still dry. Who was our deliverer in this Abaddon?

"Dave!" shouted Chris. And suddenly there he was, cowboy-hatted and spurred like some phantasmic crusader. But he was coming up from behind us. Guessing we would have problems, he had ridden from east of the pass early that morning cutting and blazing, but he'd gone down to the Moose River a different way and an easier one at that. If we had carried on up the Moose another fifty yards before turning east we would have found Dave's path and instructions from him on how to get to it. Here below the pass his good trail joined our bad one. The Marlboro Man was back in business.

Dave agreed it was a pretty poor track by all accounts, which made me feel good. If Dave says it is a poor track, it is a diabolical one. He said I'd wanted Milton's journey and I was getting it. He'd found the place in Cheadle's diary where they went through a burnt forest and it sounded no more torturous than ours:

Whole country seems to be burnt, & we shall probably have same difficulties with fallen timber for some time. Very irritating work driving horses, will fork out of the path. Can't ride after them on account of timber, dismount, whack them & chivy them back, they rushing & leaping & crashing about, I expecting they must break their legs.

The first sign Milton and Cheadle had that their journey might end was the sound of a crow. A crow is usually a bad omen but they were happy to hear this one for it meant open country ahead. Further on they found some cut branches, a faint trail, hoofprints, old marten traps. The next day they came on a trail marked with blazes and the woods opened up into a prairie. This pleased their remaining horses, which had not fed on such grass since Edmonton. They found a canoe, the print of a moccasin in the sand. Then they found a human. After what they had been through you wouldn't have thought they'd have cared what he looked like, but Milton had not lost his eye for detail:

> He came up, a most hideously repulsive-looking Indian. He wore nothing but a pair of ragged trousers, his skin was dirty, and his face perfectly diabolical – a vast expanse of visage, in the midst of which a rugged, swollen nose stood out, a mouth which yawned like the gates of Gehenna, and eyes with a most malignant squint. This monster we at once named "Caliban."

Caliban had his uses. To their questions about Kamloops he replied: "Aiyou muck-a-muck, aiyou tea, aiyou tobacco, aiyou salmon, aiyou whiskey!" The thought of which set them all salivating, although the fort was still four days away. O'Beirne took up Paley again, and a renewed optimism: "O'Beirne looked up from his book from time to time, and ventured to express a hope that we *might* escape, after all, and offered his advice upon the course to be pursued in the happier time at hand." Even Milton was persuaded to change his habits: "Saturday, August 22nd – To my astonishment Lord Milton calls me at daybreak, & we get up & make fire before rest arise, who are delighted at this change as I also. Bravo!" (Cheadle's diary)

Caliban went to fetch his friends. They must not miss this sight of stricken Englishmen emerging spectral from the woods. With their audience the travellers traded one of their shirts for rabbits and potatoes, which they immediately scoffed raw. Cheadle, with uncharacteristic lack of restraint, followed up with several handfuls of fruit of an unknown tree and suffered "such dreadful griping and feeling of sickness that I could not walk." They kept on. They traded Milton's embroidered Indian saddle for more potatoes and they stayed off the berries. Still they bickered. Two days from the fort the Assiniboine lost his temper with O'Beirne, who was being incompetent with the horses. He struck the Irishman on the head. O'Beirne, assuming again that he was being murdered, fled to Milton, declaring: "*Hic mihi nescio quod trepido male numen amicum confusam eripuit mentem.* You know, my lord, I warned you and the Doctor at Edmonton of the dangerous character you were trusting yourselves with. He is a most wicked man. I shall go on to Kamloops as soon as it is light, and get out a warrant for the apprehension of The Assiniboine immediately on his arrival." They sighted the fort on Friday, August 28, a fine hot day.

> Away we went, getting a canter out of our skeleton steeds with much difficulty. Mr O'B had walked on before the rest, in his eagerness to gain the protection of the law, and when we passed him began to run after us, crying, "Don't leave me, my lord!" "Do stop for me, Doctor! Please let me come with you!" But we had no compassion on him, and galloped on. Whenever we looked behind us, we saw Mr O'B still running at the top of his speed, afraid the blood-thirsty Assiniboine might overtake him.

They reached Kamloops in the evening, abandoned their horses and set to feasting: greasy bacon, cabbage and peas. Tobacco and tea. A meal they would remember. To Milton's delight they had arrived on the night of a ball. "Both sexes all gaudily dressed, and with some Spanish or Mexican air about them, in bright petticoats and shirts." Cheadle went to bed. Milton hung around to show off to the women, imagining his wild look would get them swooning. Instead they treated him like an exhibit in a hall of biological curiosities. He was not dressed for courting: "In truth we were as miserable and unprepossessing a company as ever presented itself for approval: our clothes in tatters, the legs of Milton's trousers torn off above the knees, and Cheadle's in ribbons; our feet covered only by the shreds of moccasins;

our faces gaunt, haggard, and unshaven; our hair long, unkempt, and matted." No one could quite believe that they had done it all for *pleasure*.

In the muted valleys the snow still fell, lightly we stepped there. This mutinous column subdued. Through subalpine meadows ran waters dark as obsidian, a world in black and white. A landscape transmogrified by retinal alchemy, a netherworld fairyland. It betrays the passing of its folk. There went bear and deer, there the coyote, there the lightly trod. They have gone before us. Now the only movement is ours. Where are they hid? They are stilled into the landscape, sculpted in ice and rock about. They have crossed the portal and they beckon us follow. There in utter desolation does great beauty lie, there beside the fringes of a great depression. In a free world do men always find ways of imprisoning themselves. Which path will you take? Will you hold to this liberation, carry on through the snows of Avalon forevermore? Or is this valley only for passing through?

Chris says the hills change her every time. I wasn't sure how they changed the Marlboro Man. Milton seemed his happiest in them. It's up to you whether they change you and how. It's all to do with how you take to the freedom. It's not as easy as it sounds to let your mind run with the hills, but I didn't want to leave them.

On it snowed, and each morning we shook out of it and set forth like subterranean creatures surface-bound for the first time. Moving south from the headwaters of the Snaring River we crossed two more passes with the mountains of the great Dividing Range to the west, and we dropped into the forest with the snow driving up on the wind. Teal passed quick-winged overhead and it was very cold. The snow froze on the stirrups and they would not hold a boot and they hung loose. We spent the night in mountain luxury in a warden's cabin at Miette Lake, a secluded heather-bound lake held in an elbow of hills and out of which the Miette River runs into the Jasper valley. It is Dave's favourite spot in the Rockies. The cabin is a regular ranger's place with a wood-burning stove and basic domesticities and a library of ranger's paperbacks: *A Bargain in Bullets, Ambush at Three Rivers, Forced March to Loon Creek, Red Runs the River, Long-Rider.* In such fantasies does the Wild West live on. In that cabin we finished our rum.

My last day in the mountains was as hard-riding as any. Even the Marlboro Man had trouble keeping his Marlboro Horse on the trail. On a precipice path, Flair stumbled as the edge gave way and Dave had his feet out of the stirrups ready to jump and we were all set for a right old rodeo. We were banged against trees and rocks and Comanche was lurching about but he never fell. For all his feeding, I could trust him anywhere. We dropped down into a different country with aspen and poplars among the spruce, and Labrador tea, buffaloberry and late-ripening fruit. It was warmer and I could feel the land breathe out as we came from the subalpine freeze. We were back in the comfort zone. We reached the valley bottom and we turned back east towards the Yellowhead Pass. We heard a car for the first time in weeks; I had not realized how loud they are. The first thing I missed about the mountains was the silence.

I looked pretty outlandish. Some of the dirt didn't come out for weeks. My hair smelt of campfires and looked Neanderthal. I had a cut or a blister on every finger. My clothes would never be worn again. I just wished I had a wedding to go to, some great-aunts to shock. Next week on Vancouver Island I would be seeing Aunt Chris, a genuine great-aunt, but I'd be hard pushed to shock her with anything.

I returned to Jasper with Dave and Chris and there I said goodbye to them, Mr. and Mrs. Assiniboine reincarnate. "Goodbye Englishman," said Chris. "Don't get too much like your Lord Milton." Whatever that meant. Dave said: "Whoever Milton was he was a tough guy. To come through all that." He meant to come through the bush, but he might equally have meant to come through life. The two were congruous – Milton had to fight through life just as he fought through the bush – although they might part at their conclusions. Milton had triumphantly come through the bush, but I wasn't sure yet how to measure his life. "You didn't do so badly yourself," said Dave. A grin from beneath the wide-brimmed cowboy hat. "For an Englishman."

On the road to Kamloops – most of which I hitchhiked – I stopped off to look at the rapids on the North Thompson that Milton and Cheadle had named Porte d'Enfer and is now known as Little Hell's Gate, there being a Hell's Gate on the Fraser River. A group of American tourists had done the same, and I listened to their guide giving her history lesson. Suddenly, she started on about Milton and Cheadle. I couldn't resist, and introduced myself. The guide, a large, excitable lady who nodded a lot, said "Oh my God" about a dozen times, and then she looked as if she were going to cry. "I've been telling his story for twenty years," she wailed, thrusting me before her flock like a sinner-turned-penitent. There followed a great stirring of hornets to their prey. I tried to point out that I was merely a descendant who did not even share his name, but they had it fixed I was his heir come to claim my birthright. I played along, told them about my journey – the embellished version. Widening of eyes, sounds of Americans enthusing. I still had the Neanderthal look so my tale was all very believable.

"Did you nearly starve?"

Oh, very nearly.

"How did you survive?"

I ate my horses.

"You ate your horses?"

To the bone.

A sudden withdrawing of hornets. They looked nervously to their guide, who was nodding furiously. "Yes, well, it's been, er, an experience to meet you Lord, er, Mr. Milton, sir, something we, all of us, are going to remember I'm sure. A pleasure, Mr. Milton. I trust, ahem, you're not still hungry." Then she bowed. Then they all bowed. I stood there aghast. The hornets swung in behind their queen and off they scuttled. This was not the reaction Milton would have got – when it came to diet, those were more liberal times.

At Kamloops, Milton and Cheadle caught up on news of the world: the marriage of the Prince of Wales, the Polish insurrection, threat of war between Denmark and Prussia, the progress of the American Civil War. They bathed and rested, but all they really wanted to do was eat, which they did most of the time, if a little guiltily:

> Deal with us gently, sour ascetics and stern divines abhorring the carnal, and corpulent, virtuous magistrates who sit in judgment on miserable creatures driven into sin by starvation – *expertis credite*. Have we not thousands on our side in this great city who daily hunger? – not to mention a few aldermen and a well-fed bishop or two to back us on principle? Talk not to us of intellectual raptures; the mouth and stomach are the doors by which enter true delight.

In their three weeks at Kamloops Cheadle put on forty-one pounds.

At Kamloops they parted company with O'Beirne, not without "a certain feeling of regret," despite him demanding of them a pair of socks, a silk necktie, tea, sugar, bread and money for the road. A parasitic clown to the end. They would see him for the last time in Victoria, where he was attempting to rebuild his faith under the tutelage of the local clergy. He was later traced to Queensland, Australia. There, according to a postscript to a later edition of *The North-West Passage by Land*, he "entered again on a wandering career as peripatetic pedagogue and philosopher . . . upon occasion enlivening the bush fireside by an account of hairbreadth escapes during that terrible journey across the Rocky Mountains." With Mr. and Mrs. Assiniboine and their son still in tow, Milton and Cheadle moved out of Kamloops and rode south through Lytton, Yale and Hope and west through Langley, and caught a ferry to Victoria on Vancouver Island. They tried for a bed at the Hôtel de France whose proprietor, noting their leather shirts and singular appearance and lack of luggage, declared the place full. Indignant, they marched off. They had not got far before a waiter caught up with them and begged them return. The proprietor had discovered who they were. Milton, rarely spurned, was unimpressed: "We turned a deaf ear, and continued on our way to the St. George, where we found capital accommodation, and having properly refreshed ourselves, took the rough hint we had received, and betook ourselves to the nearest tailor, to obtain more civilised attire."

They were in Victoria to indulge themselves, and to be fêted by the Hudson's Bay Company governor, James Douglas, and other local dignitaries. They were also there to indulge the Assiniboines – to introduce them "to the wonders of civilisation."

We clothed them in gorgeous apparel, seated them in a "buggy" drawn by a pair of fast-trotting horses, and mounting the box ourselves, drove them in state to Esquimalt [the harbour]. They sat inside with great gravity, occasionally remarking on the difference between bowling along a capital road at the rate we were going, and advancing only two or three miles a day, by hard labour, through the forest.

They took them on HMSS *Sutlej*, where they dined with the Admiral. They took them shopping. Then they took them to the theatre, an occasion that may or may not have been the subject of the following story from that time in *The Colonist*, a local newspaper:

SMOKING IN THE THEATRE – A young man, who for once shall be nameless, rendered himself both conspicuous and disagreeable last evening in the dress circle of the theatre by puffing vigorously on a cheroot, to the evident disgust of several ladies seated near him. This breach of the rules of common decency is totally inexcusable.

Was it the Assiniboine? Was it Milton?

The Assiniboines would spend that winter in Kamloops and recross the Rockies by the Kootenay Pass the following summer with a string of horses. A few weeks later in Edmonton the Assiniboine, that "brave, indomitable, and matchless guide . . . who had endured without injury so many hardships, and combatted with such wonderful resource and skill the great difficulties which beset us in our journey," contracted smallpox or some other disease of European origin and died. It seemed an unworthy end. His son became a guide and, Milton noted, "retained the somewhat unruly disposition and capacity for driving pack-horses which distinguished him when in our service."

Milton and Cheadle felt they could not return to England without having seen the goldfields, so at the end of September 1963 they each donned jackboots, rolled a spare shirt, pair of socks and toothbrush into a blanket and set off "miners' fashion" to Cariboo. In the wayside houses of this new El Dorado they encountered vile alcoholic brews, miners of various nationalities and rumours of the peripatetic O'Beirne, who had passed through on his circuitous way to Victoria and apparently drunk into a coma anyone who had challenged him:

> If their heads were hard, Mr O'B's was harder, and although he had not tasted any intoxicating liquor for two years, and drank glass for glass with his entertainers without shirking, he proved invincible. One after another the conspirators subsided helpless on the floor, while Mr O'B remained sitting, smiling and triumphant, and calmly continued to smoke his pipe, superior and alone!

They also encountered card games, blasphemy and slang unknown to them: "bully for you," "caved in," "played out," "you bet," "you bet your life," "your bottom dollar," "your gumboots on it," "on the make," "on the sell," "a big strike," "can't get a show," "hit a streak." It was language certain to tighten the corsets at Wentworth. The Cariboo was no place for airs and graces, as Milton found out one evening at a hotel when "in a weak and absent moment" he astonished their fellow residents by "mechanically" placing his boots outside his bedroom door expecting them to be cleaned. He was roundly abused. "Who is this — fellow putting on frills?"

The Cariboo in the 1860s was the land of the free, in the sense that anyone was free to go there. The usual social mores did not apply. A criminal's dollar was as good as a clergyman's. Compared with Victorian England it was like running naked in the rain. It was tough and unsophisticated. Gold replaced furs as the new currency of the West, which unsettled the Hudson's Bay Company. The vast majority of those who came seeking their fortunes never found them, and many of those who did squandered them. Milton encountered a miner who had dug $40,000 of gold in a single summer and spent it all in the bars of Victoria by the following spring. In one bar this prodigal treated the entire clientele to champagne, and when that failed to exhaust the stock invited people in off the street. There remained champagne undrunk, so he instructed the barman to fill every glass and place them on the counter, from where he swept them to the floor with his stick. Still a case lay intact. This he dispatched by stamping on the bottles in his heavy boots. He was one fool among many. Milton also recalled a miner from California who, lost as to how he might use his fortune, substituted the wooden pins in a bowling alley for full bottles of champagne, "smashing batch after batch with infinite satisfaction to himself, amid the applause of his companions."

Through this assembly of disparates marched the Englishmen, and in no other society would Milton feel so free. He and Cheadle took their places in the carnival. Milton was shaved by Mr. Dixie, a black barber from Tennessee, who insisted he would die happy only if he could shave a real, live lord. He washed gold from the Fraser, and he would use it later in his wedding ring. On their last night in Cariboo a dinner was held in their honour in the ward of the local hospital. The single unfortunate patient was veiled from view by a sheet. The company was Dr. Black, the host; Mr. Cocker, manager of a local bank; Mr. Blenkinsopp, a Hudson's Bay Company man; Dr. Bell, a physician; Mr. Courtney, an Irish lawyer; Billy the Bladge, a successful miner; and Mrs. Morris, "fair, fat and forty." (In *The North-West Passage by Land* these names are disguised, as are the names of all the characters in the book except their own and those whom Milton did not consider gentlemen, including women.) They feasted rather incongruously on soup, roast beef, boiled mutton, plum pudding and champagne, and there followed toasts of deep solemnity to the "illustrious travellers."

Dr B——l, who had shown symptoms of restlessness for some time, could repress the flood of eloquence rising within him no longer, and having succeeded in catching the president's eye, and received a permissive nod in return, rose cautiously on his legs. A vigorous rapping on the table procured silence, and Dr B——l, steadying himself by the table with one tremulous hand, and waving the other gracefully towards ourselves, proposed Milton's health in most glowing terms, winding up his panegyric with a request for three-times-three, and "He's a jolly good fellow." These were given uproariously.

Thereafter Dr. B——l rose every few minutes to toast Milton – "the Noble Scion of one of the noblest houses England ever produced" – and each time was sung down by the multitude. He was rendered mute and gloomy, until "all at once he got up, and rushing across the room, made ineffectual attempts to force an exit through the mantelpiece, bobbing against it very much after the fashion of a bird trying to escape through a pane of glass; whereupon he was seized by the assistant, and led off to a bedroom."

They returned to Victoria, where Cheadle read the papers and Milton partied. In that city, days before they started the journey by boat back to England and without his usual premonitory symptoms, Milton suffered two epileptic fits, triggered perhaps by sweet thoughts of home. Before leaving for England he prepared for his return, buying seven small lots of land at £20 to £30 each at New Westminster, south of present-day Vancouver – a laying-down of new-found roots and great hopes for his future here. Cheadle records him being "carried away by the excitement" of the sale. "Milton bid against me by mistake, and I of course stopped bidding, therefore did not buy at all." All I know about Milton's land is that he still owned it on October 29, 1865, and that his family does not own it now.

They sailed out towards San Francisco via the San Juan Islands, the subject of a United States–Canada border dispute and soon to be the subject of Milton's second book. Christmas Day 1863 they spent at sea, and carried on down the west coast of America to Panama and then to New York "with the languid carelessness of lotos-eaters." They slept a lot, Milton more than most. He was elected president of the boat's "Owl Club." They met women, Milton more than most. He considered them "exceedingly pretty, but nearly all with the usual failing of the women of this continent, rather too flat chested and without that lovely roundness of form and limb so characteristic of our girls at home." A connoisseur casting judgement. On March 5, 1864, Milton and Cheadle disembarked in Liverpool, one year, eight months and fourteen days after they set out, and they landed into a different world entirely.

EXILE

Into the ring stepped Milton, back to face his demons and detractors. He must have been apprehensive, given how he had left things two years earlier. You do not mend a broken cup by leaving it. But a lot had happened since then, and he was received in England like a conquering hero. Cheadle was too, but Milton's was the first name on the book and his was the one the societies wanted on their lecture programs.

It had been, after all, a remarkable journey. The Rev. G. Grant, a member of Sandford Fleming's surveying party that followed Milton's route along the North Thompson River in 1872, was astonished that the Englishmen survived it. "Had they but known it," he wrote in *Ocean to Ocean*, "they were beaten as completely as, by the rules of war, the British troops were beaten at Waterloo. They should have submitted to the inevitable, and starved." They were held up as classic English heroes, fêted by everyone from the Royal Geographical Society to Fleet Street.

Milton had hardly stepped off the boat from North America when he was dispatched on a nationwide lecture tour. He spoke before every audience from the Royal Geographical Society in London and the British Association in Bath to the Rotherham Mechanics' Institute and the Barnsley Young Men's Christian Association. Still only twenty-five, he seduced his audiences with stories of improbable audacity, and he was full of theories as to what was likely to happen to the Wild West and what had gone before. The English loved their heroes and they took to this one. A member of the panel at one of his lectures compared Milton rather generously to Lord Cardigan, who led the charge of the Light Brigade at Balaclava in the Crimean War, declaring that should England ever want another hero to take Lord Cardigan's place, he was sure the noble lecturer would not shrink from such a calling. Sir Roderick Murchison, president of the British Association and of the Royal Geographical Society, applauded him for "leaving the ease and luxury of a home like his for the true advance-ment of science." Sir John Richardson, who accompanied Sir John Franklin on two of his arctic expeditions, remarked that "so long as in the cause of science the nobility showed such skill, enterprise, and perseverance, as that of Viscount Milton, England might be proud of her aristocracy." My favourite commentary is from the *Illustrated Times*:

Lord Milton is something better than a Lord; he has proved himself to be a fine, heroic young man, of true English pluck and daring. He has lately crossed the Rocky Mountains to discover whether a north-western passage by land from the Atlantic to the Pacific be not possible that way; in his journey he had to confront difficulties and brave dangers which might well have appalled a much older and more experienced traveller. Lord Milton is, then, no listless, shiftless Lord Dundreary, neither is he a mere pleasure-hunter, but a genuine Englishman – a splinter off the old Hartz rock – brave, tough, wise, energetic, and shifty in expedients.

On they eulogized:

There are few stories . . . of British pluck and endurance, so exciting, so interesting, and so memorable, as that of the North-West passage by land achieved by Lord Milton. (*Temple Bar*)

We needed not the records of the Alpine Club . . . to prove that Englishmen are as adventurous as ever, and as fond of testing their muscular development in untried fields. (*The London Review*)

One of the best books of travel that we have ever read. (*The Athenaeum*)

The first thing that tempts us after reading such a book is to exclaim *cui bono?* – for what reason on earth was a journey of such utter suffering, hardship and peril ever willingly undertaken? The only answer is that the men who undertook it were Englishmen. (*The Standard*)

Milton and Cheadle outlined their reasons for the journey in the preface to *The North-West Passage by Land*:

The Authors have been anxious to give a faithful account of their travels and adventures amongst the prairies, forests, and mountains of the Far West. . . . But one of the principal objects they have had in view has been to draw attention to the vast importance of establishing a highway from the Atlantic to the Pacific through the British possessions. . . .

The favourite scheme of geographers in this country for the last three centuries has been the discovery of a North-West Passage by sea, as the shortest route to the rich countries of the East. The discovery has been made, but in a commercial point of view it has proved valueless. We have attempted to show that . . . the true North-West Passage is by land.

For all the imperialistic bombast, people liked the book above all because Milton and Cheadle appeared to have done the journey just for the hell of it. Anyone who plunged into the wilds of Canada, declared the *Pall Mall Gazette*, would have to have "a poetical love of adventure." It was just so terribly English. Foreign reviewers were nonplussed. "*Il a toute l'énergie de sa race*," was all one Parisian commentator could come up with in analysis of Milton's motives. A paper published by the Hudson's Bay Company in Canada described the book as "difficult." Difficult to believe, perhaps. But the English audience had no difficulty in taking to it. It went into five editions in eight months. The ninth and final edition was published in 1901, thirty-six years after the first and twenty-four years after Milton's death.

What did his family think of it all? There is no record, although *The Times* reckoned that

> a Lord Fitzwilliam of the eighteenth century, could he return to our sublunary sphere, would be amazed at the volume now before us. What could he, whose "grand tour" had been a visit to a few polished capitals of Europe, to become versed in their manners and vices, think of a descendant who had "crossed North America into British Columbia through one of the passes of the Rocky Mountains?"

It wasn't, apparently, a very Fitzwilliam thing to do. Then again, Milton did not sound like a very Fitzwilliam Fitzwilliam.

The only critical noises came after the publication of Cheadle's diary in 1931 from Canadian historians who seem to have had it in for Milton because he was a viscount. Claiming to have read between the lines of the diary they nail him as a "spoiled young sprig of nobility," "obstinate, with a weak man's frightening tenacity," "arrogant, lazy and temperamental" and, best of all, "irresponsible and soft-hearted, with a fondness for good rum and for pretty women not necessarily good." He might have agreed with the last bit.

In the wake of this success Milton stepped for a while into the life expected of him. Perhaps it was the one he would have wanted, all things being equal. He was elected as a Liberal MP in 1865, the year *The North-West Passage by Land* was published. He held his seat until 1872, but he was never quite committed to it the way his father had been. He was always reminiscing about Canada, always looking west, even in the House of Commons. To the consternation of his constituents in Yorkshire, nearly two-thirds of his contributions on the floor of the Commons concerned British Columbia or the Red River Settlement.

He had given several reasons in *The North-West Passage by Land* why he thought his Yellowhead route was the best for a railway: proximity to the goldfields, gentle gradients, fordable rivers, friendly Indians. But the one he considered the most important was its distance from the American frontier – it was a good four degrees of latitude north. He was not particularly keen on Americans and he did not trust the United States government. Milton's second book, published like his first by Cassell, Petter, and Galpin in London but paid for by him, was about the dispute between the United States and Britain over the border separating British Columbia and the American mainland. The Oregon Treaty of 1846 gave the United States possession of everything south of the forty-ninth parallel and extended the boundary through the middle of the channel between Vancouver Island and the mainland, but it left unsettled the ownership of San Juan Island, which lies in the middle of that channel.

Both countries claimed it. In June 1859 an American settler shot a pig belonging to the Hudson's Bay Company that had been digging in his garden, and the subsequent posturing almost brought Britain and the United States to war.

Milton's *A History of the San Juan Water Boundary Question* came out in 1869, while the island was under joint military occupation, and it is not a gripping read. "I need offer no apology for laying this statement before the Public," begins Milton apologetically. There follow 446 pages of letters and documents that had passed between and within the American and British governments on this matter, along with Milton's hermetic commentary. He tried to show how conceding San Juan Island to the United States would weaken Britain's power base in the Pacific and force British Columbia and afterwards Saskatchewan, not then a part of Canada, into the U.S. federation. "Canada, excluded from the Pacific, and shut in on two sides by United States territory, must eventually follow the same course," he warned.

His parliamentary colleagues were bemused by his Canadian obsession. "Having listened for some time to the statement of the noble Viscount I am really at a loss to understand the object he has in view," conceded one minister faced with a question from Milton about the effectiveness of British Columbia's postal service. When he was not satisfied by an answer – and he rarely was – Milton would merely ask the question again another time. His demand for the government to "lay upon the Table of the House the letters, despatches and enclosures addressed to the Foreign

Office by Governor Douglas [of British Columbia] . . . informing Her Majesty's Government of the intention of the United States Forces to invade part or parts of Her Majesty's Possessions in the Pacific" he repeated four times without result. He appears to have become a rampant colonialist, even by the anti-American standards of the day.

By the time the final edition of *The North-West Passage by Land* was published Canada had a trans-national railway, but it did not cross the Yellowhead Pass. The Canadian Pacific Railway runs across the prairies just north of the American border and crosses the Rocky Mountains through the Kicking Horse Pass, well to the south of Jasper. Perhaps it was just as well for Milton that he was not alive to see it built. But if he had lived into his seventies, he would have had the satisfaction of seeing a second line open on almost exactly the route he and Cheadle had taken through the Yellowhead and down the North Thompson River. A road was later built alongside it, first traversed in its roughest form in 1923 by Charles Grant and Frank Mitchell in a Model-T Ford. It was vindication, though belated.

Milton's vision for San Juan Island was less prophetic. In 1871 the matter was referred for arbitration to Kaiser Wilhelm I of Germany, who in October the following year ruled in favour of the United States. British Columbia and Saskatchewan did not follow suit, and Canada remained forever Canadian. The subject of Milton's political obsession would be remembered for a contretemps involving a pig.

❖

Perhaps he sensed which way Kaiser Wilhelm would rule. Perhaps his epilepsy had got worse, though the treatments had improved. Perhaps, as a Canadian newspaper called the *Daily Colonist* suggested, he was harbouring "an extreme distaste for the exigencies of his position as a country member, the heir to a great title and to the position of one of the greatest of English landowners." For whatever reason, in the spring of 1872 Milton decided that the role mapped out for him in England, which he had tried to fill in the noble Fitzwilliam tradition of politics, was not working. Contained once more by the Fitzwilliam straitjacket and haunted maybe by memories of North American horizons, he took his wife, Laura – who was pregnant – and their two daughters, Laura and Mabel, and left England for good.

They sailed to Canada and rented an isolated wooden farmhouse north of Lake Superior at a bend on the Kaministiquia River known as Pointe de Meuron, where a reconstruction of the Hudson's Bay Company outpost of Fort William now stands. In this place in 1816 Milton's kinsman Lord Selkirk and his band of mercenaries, hired from a Colonel De Meuron's Swiss Regiment to protect Selkirk's Red River Settlement, camped to confront his enemies across the river at the North West Company outpost of Fort William. Milton may even have felt some empathy with Selkirk, holed up in that wilderness in defiance of his antagonists.

The house was owned by John McIntyre, Hudson's Bay Company chief trader at Fort William. It was described by one writer as "very rough," by another as "of an uncouth and somewhat uncomfortable degree of civilization." Compared with Wentworth Woodhouse it probably was, but compared with that house what wasn't? It was lonely, but Milton was used to that. Laura spent the time reviving the old art of cut-work needle lace, or *punto tagliato*, for which she made quite a name in those parts, teaching McIntyre's daughter and helping her design her trousseau. Then on July 25, in the presence of their personal doctor, Thomas Miller, who had accompanied them from England, Laura gave birth to a son. An Ontario newspaper announced the birth and fantasized: "The cries of the young stranger will be echoed by those of Indian papooses, and the tender sympathy of the tawny squaws in their wigwams, with the coronetted mother in her tent, will show a touch of nature which makes the whole world kin." How Milton would have liked that. William Charles De Meuron Wentworth-Fitzwilliam was his wilderness baby, and no Fitzwilliam heir had been born so far from Wentworth. How he would have liked that too.

Milton was back where he seemed to belong, in the Canadian wilderness, though he had not left all his demons behind. One day later that summer he took Billy for a walk. But when he got back to the house he no longer had the child with him, indeed he could not even recollect taking him out. Laura, vexed, raised a search party, which eventually found the infant unharmed on a haystack. Milton, it transpired, had suffered an epileptic fit while walking and had placed Billy on the haystack for safekeeping when he realized what was happening. Such was the intensity of his fit that when he came round he had forgotten all about him.

This story reached Wentworth, and it is clear from how they used it just what Milton had been up against in that household. After his death in 1877, Billy by law became heir to the Fitzwilliam earldom, but Milton's brothers contested his eligibility, claiming that Milton and Laura had picked up the wrong baby that day at Pointe de Meuron and that the Billy before them was not his real son. This happened when Billy and his uncles were all living together at Wentworth. There's no place like home. The uncles dropped the case only when their solicitor absconded with some of their money. It was as absurd as it sounds: Billy had all the attributes expected of a Fitzwilliam – including the goatish instincts of his father and grandfather.

A few months after the haystack incident, Milton's farm-house at Pointe de Meuron burnt down, very nearly with all of them inside. Milton was never dull to be with. They decamped to another outback hideaway near Richmond, Virginia. Why Virginia? I have no idea, and neither do I have any idea what they did there. After leaving British Columbia I spent a week in Richmond and found no trace of Milton ever having been there, though I had enough information from my grandmother to know that he was, from 1872 until he died, and that Laura stayed on well after that: she left their Virginia house in her will to two of her sisters. Milton and his family reportedly lived there under an assumed name. It was a self-imposed exile of the afflicted. Illness abounded. But there was freedom and hunting, and no politics.

Although I didn't know Milton's assumed name, I expected to find out something about him in Richmond.

I came away with nothing. It was the most depressing moment in two years of research. His last five years are a biographical black hole. Hundreds of hours in libraries and archives and hundreds of miles of travelling and I had little more than what I started with: one fabulous mystery. I was disappointed then, but I am not disappointed now. A family legend tells you much about that family, not through the truth of the matter but through the mythology. What parts of the story at the expense of other parts has it held to itself and why? Demystifying Milton would have been like trying to analyze a favourite poem. Sometimes it's better to run with the thing. For my grandmother, Milton's story had been all about a great adventure of almost mythic quality. It could have been about all kinds of things but that was what it meant to her. For me it was about an adventure and about freedom, it was about changing and seeing how the people around you took to that. My brother or my sisters or my cousins might each have their own take on the story, but that is mine and that is what I'll tell. This is why the greatest family legends are living legends and why they are so important. They tell you about the people who have passed them on.

Milton died at 6 a.m. on Wednesday, January 17, 1877, aged thirty-seven, in Rouen, France. I have no idea what he was doing there but he had been lying ill there for some weeks. Consistent with his other rites of passage there appears to be no record of how he died. Had he died in England, the cause of his death would be on his official death certificate. Consular death certificates, inevitably, record only the place. It was a fitting sign-off. His death may have been to do with his epilepsy or it may have been to do with something else entirely. It is just another mystery in the life and death of this mystery-man. "Thus for the second time in the memory of many still living, the House of Wentworth has lost by death its eldest son," reflected the *Sheffield Independent*. Milton was buried at Wentworth, though hardly with the ceremony usually reserved for eldest sons of distinguished Houses. The *Rotherham and Masbro' Advertiser* noted:

The whole of the proceedings were of a very quiet and unostentatious nature, and formed a touching contrast to the usual pomp of the funerals of the aristocracy. This was in accordance with the expressed wish of Earl and Countess Fitzwilliam, and there was little to indicate the exalted position of him to whose memory the last tribute was being paid. . . . The [funereal] route was the shortest and most private which could be chosen, more than half of it being through the gardens at the back of Wentworth House, and the work of the bearers was consequently much lighter than it would have been had the road through the Park and the village been selected.

They tried to sneak him out the back way. How delightfully appropriate, as is his epitaph on his tomb in the Fitzwilliam mausoleum:

Fear not for I have redeemed thee,
I have called thee by thy name,
Thou art mine. (Isaiah XLIII)

The wayward son was absolved only in death. He is contained by concrete and biblical judgement in that damp
subterranean catacomb, entombed beside Charles, his
father's elder brother – another Viscount Milton who died
prematurely – and Charles's stillborn son. The eradication
of the first seeds. It is as gloomy as it sounds down there.
Laura was laid next to him nine years later. Surely they
would have preferred a hilltop grave in some North
American wilderness, attended by Indians and the cycles of
the Moon.

EPILOGUE

The last thing I did in Canada was stay with my great-aunt Chris in her bungalow in Black Creek, halfway up the east coast of Vancouver Island. Staying with Aunt Chris is more unpredictable than taking a string of horses through the Rockies.

She picked me up from Campbell River airport in her camper-van. Beside her sat Kelsey, her beloved English bulldog. Kelsey goes everywhere with Aunt Chris. "Seatbelt!" she bellowed as we careered southwards, always a sensible option when travelling with her as she comes from the same school of driving as my grandmother. She, of course, refuses to wear one. Her excuse whenever the police stop her, which is often, is always the same: she has just finished clearing up a pool of dog-sick. With Kelsey in the passenger seat, that always appears plausible. Aunt Chris moved to Black Creek only recently, but she is making a name for herself with her van. The week before I arrived, she was pulled over by the police after an alarmed motorist reported it veering across the road like a thing possessed. She had been trying to swat a wasp. She made a name for herself at her old home, too. A few years ago, in her late seventies, she and a friend competed in a seven-hour charity rally around Salt Spring Island dressed as nuns. Two more unlikely candidates for the sisterhood never existed.

On the way back to her house from the airport we were talking so much she seemed to forget about the driving and oblivious to the long line of cars behind her she hardly exceeded twenty miles an hour. She wanted to know everything about my journey, down to where we watered the horses. She said she once had a horse called Comanche. I showed her some photographs and warned that my horses probably looked rough compared to the Arabs she used to breed, and she looked over them and picked out their good points and considered them rather well suited to the task. Her horses, she said, would have broken their necks or mine in the first mile. "They would have tripped over a dandelion and spooked if you'd sneezed." Aunt Chris knows what she is talking about with horses. In an old newspaper cutting she is described as "the outstanding Arab breeder in Canada." She sold one of her stallions for C$1 million. She has trophies and a large box of rosettes. She has Laura Milton's silver-buttoned riding jacket in black and Fitzwilliam green that

Laura wore when hunting in Virginia. Like Milton, Aunt Chris could ride almost as soon as she could walk.

It wasn't just my horses that interested her. Aunt Chris has a copy of *The North-West Passage by Land* and she would have liked to have followed Milton herself, but she was not told about the book until she was past thirty and by then she was married. Grandma always said her sister went to Canada because of Milton, but Aunt Chris didn't know about him until she had emigrated. She had followed him unwittingly; the trail of the outcast leads West. So much of what she says could have been said by Milton. It all comes down to family. She moved to Canada in her late twenties to get away from her stern mother – "I always felt she was embarrassed to have me around." She has never visited her mother's grave, and she will not. She also moved to get away from what she calls the worst of English society: the stuffiness, the secrecy, the rumours. The Fitzwilliams were dreadful for all that, she says. They created a world of intrigue that prevented people from knowing too much. Aunt Chris would rather it was all up front. If there's something to tell she'll tell it. You won't find her saying one thing to someone's face and another behind their back. This makes her entertaining to be with. "Did I order a car accident?" she bellowed to a startled waiter who brought her borscht at lunch the next day. It was the sort of thing my grandmother would have said, though Aunt Chris said it louder.

There are some things she misses about England, though they have never been enough to pull her back. She misses the politeness and what she calls "standards." She misses her close family and she misses her sister. She chose her bungalow in Black Creek because it is pink, the same colour as Grandma's house in Hampshire. When Grandma died, Aunt Chris was ill and could not fly back for her funeral so she makes me take her through it all, and through her dying. She ponders it deeply. It was just how their mother had gone. She talks about my father and when he visited her in Canada before he died, and how the last time she saw him he was standing in a boat headed for Vancouver driven by a group of drunks and "B," as she called him, in his city suit waving from among the cowboy hats and beer cans and loving it all. She reckoned he'd be pleased about my Milton trip. She is pleased about my Milton trip. "About time someone else in this family did something unconventional." I said when it came to unconventional I'd never be able to compete with her. We got out her copy of *The North-West Passage by Land*. Aunt Chris is convinced Cheadle was a drunk. "He had a swig at every river, that's what I heard." I cannot imagine how she came to that conclusion but Aunt Chris's stories, like my grandmother's, while obscurely sourced are rarely completely made up.

In her house Aunt Chris has pictures and mementoes of her old English life, and especially of her father. Every night at supper that week we had napkins held in rings and she cooked roast beef, chicken, English stuffing. On my birthday she cooked me a large chocolate cake. We talked a lot about England. She does not much like Americans. She is quite old-fashioned and does not enjoy technology. Her house is full of gadgets she cannot work. She complains her telephone answer-machine makes the place look like the cockpit of a Boeing 747. But Aunt Chris is not an Englishwoman abroad. Her children are Canadian. She speaks with a Canadian accent. She drinks milk with rye, claiming anything weaker disagrees with her. She congratulated me on not being too English: "No buttons on your sleeves, shirt hanging out, things falling off your rucksack, I am delighted, Michael. Just wait until I tell your mother." She also has Kelsey, as unconventional a pet as you are likely to find. Kelsey is too fat to scratch her ear. With much grunting she goes through the motions but she paws only air. She is not an active dog. She cannot make it into the camper-van without a footstool. Aunt Chris pampers her unashamedly. In the supermarket in Black Creek we bought ham for ourselves and beef heart for Kelsey. But then she is a pedigree bulldog, and a valuable one. She requires the full treatment. Aunt Chris is as successful a breeder of bulldogs as she was of horses.

I am proud of my Aunt Chris because of the difficult choices she has made in trying to follow a path that is true for her. She inspires me to believe that I can do it too, that anyone can. So much of what I saw in Milton I see in her. Milton, like her, made his difficult choices with great courage. What he had to overcome and what Aunt Chris has had to, I can only guess at. Given Milton's vulnerabilities and what he was born into, he is twice the legend I started off with.

She put me on a bus to Vancouver for my flight back to England and she worried where I'd stay. I told her I knew a hotel for $45 a night. "*Dar*ling," she said, "it must be a brothel." It was sad leaving Aunt Chris because I didn't know when I'd see her again. Now Grandma has died there isn't much to draw her to England. She prefers to go to Mexico. She is as exiled as Milton was, except she hasn't so far seen fit to change her name. She misses things but there is no going back. There are many great things about her and one of the best is her energy. "Growing old is not much fun," she wrote me the following year. "One way to deal with it is to get bloody-minded and meet the challenge. So far I seem to be winning." This sweet-grass trail is long and difficult and many have stepped there and many will follow.

SOURCES CONSULTED

Personal correspondence and documents relating to Milton and the Fitzwilliams are taken from the Wentworth Woodhouse Muniments at Sheffield Archives, cited with the kind permission of the Head of Leisure Services at Sheffield City Council and the trustees of the Rt. Hon. Olive Countess Fitzwilliam's Chattels Settlement; the Northamptonshire County Records Office at Wootton Hall Park, Northampton; the library at Trinity College, University of Cambridge; the library at the Victoria and Albert Museum in London; the Eton College library, courtesy of Mrs. Hatfield and Tim Card; and from private sources.

Newspaper and journal extracts and other documents relating to Milton's journey were researched at the following institutions:

CANADA – British Columbia Archives, Victoria; Manuscript Division, National Archives of Canada, Ottawa; Ethnology Division, Canadian Museum of Civilization, Ottawa; Hudson's Bay Company Archives, Provincial Archives of Manitoba, Winnipeg; Thunder Bay Historical Museum Society; Special Collections, University of Calgary Libraries; Glenbow Museum Archives, Calgary; Edmonton City Archives; library at Fort Edmonton Park.

ENGLAND – Royal Geographical Society, London; Bodleian Library, University of Oxford; Rotherham City Library; Minton China archives in Stoke-on-Trent.

Adamson, Donald, and Beauclerk-Dewar, Peter, *The House of Nell Gwyn*, London, Kimber, 1974.

Ballantyne, Robert M., *Hudson's Bay*, London, William Blackwood, 1848.

Begg, Alexander, *History of the North-West*, Toronto, Hunter and Rose, 1894.

Brown, George W., *Building the Canadian Nation*, London, J. M. Dent, 1944.

Bryce, George, *A Short History of the Canadian People*, London, Sampson Low, 1887.

Chambers's *Encyclopaedia*, 1895.

Cheadle, Walter Butler, *Cheadle's Journal of Trip across Canada, 1862–1863*, Ottawa, Graphic, 1931.

Country Life publications, *Wentworth Woodhouse* (booklet), 1924.

de Lasteyrie, Jules, "La Territoire de la Compagnie de la Baie d'Hudson," in *Revue des deux mondes*, 1867.

Dempsey, Hugh A., *Big Bear: The End of Freedom*, Vancouver, Douglas and McIntyre, 1984.

Dion, Joseph F., *My Tribe the Crees*, ed. Hugh Dempsey, Calgary, Glenbow Museum, 1979.

Gadd, Ben, *Handbook of the Canadian Rockies*, Jasper, Corax Press, 1995.

Gibbon, John Murray, *Steel of Empire*, New York, The Bobbs-Merrill Company, 1935.

Hansard's Parliamentary Debates, 1865 (vol. 177) to 1872 (vol. 210), London, Cornelius Buck.

Hargrave, Joseph James, *Red River*, Montreal, John Lovell, 1871.

Henry, Alexander the Elder, *Travels and Adventures*, New York, Riley, 1809.

Hill, Douglas, *The Opening of the Canadian West*, London, Heinemann, 1967.

Hind, Henry Youle, *Narrative of the Canadian Red River Exploring Expedition of 1857 and of the Assiniboine and Saskatchewan Exploring Expedition of 1858*, Toronto, 1859.

Howse, Geoffrey, *Around Hoyland*, Stroud, Gloucestershire, Sutton Publishing, 1999.

Lechtenberg, Richard, *Epilepsy and the Family*, Cambridge, Massachusetts, Harvard University Press, 1984.

Macdonald, Norman, *Canada: Immigration and Colonization, 1841–1903*, Aberdeen University Press, 1966.

MacGregor, J. G., *Overland by the Yellowhead*, Saskatoon, Western Producer Prairie Books, 1974.

MacLaren, I. S., *The Influence of Eighteenth-Century British Landscape Aesthetics on Narrative and Pictorial Responses to the British North American North and West, 1769–1872*, Ph.D. thesis, University of Western Ontario, 1983.

McMicking, Thomas, *Overland from Canada to British Columbia*, Vancouver, University of British Columbia Press, 1981.

Mee, Graham, *Aristocratic Enterprise: The Fitzwilliam Industrial Undertakings, 1795–1857*, Glasgow, Blackie, 1975.

Messiter, Charles Alston, *Sport and Adventures among the North-American Indians*, London, R. II. Porter, 1890.

Milton, Viscount, and Cheadle, W. B., *The North-West Passage by Land*, London, Cassell, Petter and Galpin, 1865.

Milton, Viscount, *A History of the San Juan Water Boundary Question*, London, Cassell, Petter and Galpin, 1869.

Morton, Arthur S., *A History of the Canadian West to 1870–71*, London, Thomas Nelson, 1939.

Morton, W. L., *Manitoba: A History*, University of Toronto Press, 1957.

Peat, F. David, *The Blackwinged Night*, Cambridge, Massachusetts, Perseus, 2000.

Piniuta, Harry, *Land of Pain, Land of Promise*, Saskatoon, Western Producer Prairie Books, 1978.

Porter, Roy, *The Greatest Benefit to Mankind*, London, HarperCollins, 1997.

Russell, Loris, *Everyday Life in Colonial Canada*, London, Batsford, 1973.

Sampson, Connie, *Blinded by Silence*, Edmonton, NeWest Press, 1995.

Searle, Ronald, and Dobbs, Kildare, *The Great Fur Opera*, London, Dennis Dobson, 1970.

Shortt, Adam, and Doughty, Arthur G. (ed.), *Canada and Its Provinces*, Toronto, Publishers' Association of Canada, 1913–17.

Smith, E. A., *Whig Principles and Party Politics: Earl Fitzwilliam and the Whig Party, 1748–1833*, Manchester University Press, 1975.

Stutevant, William (ed.), *Handbook of North American Indians*, Washington, D.C., Smithsonian Institution, 1978.

Temkin, Owsei, *The Falling Sickness: A History of Epilepsy from the Greeks to the Beginnings of Modern Neurology*, Baltimore, Maryland, Johns Hopkins Press, 1971.

Thompson, David, *David Thompson's Narrative, 1784–1812*, Toronto, The Champlain Society, 1962.

Wade, Mark Sweeten, *The Overlanders of '62*, Victoria, Archives of British Columbia, 1931.

Wright, Richard and Rochelle, *Yellowhead Mileposts*, Vancouver, Mitchell Press, 1975.